AF335666

# *the* Gymnastics *of* Love & Discipline

*A parental template for giving children a voice*

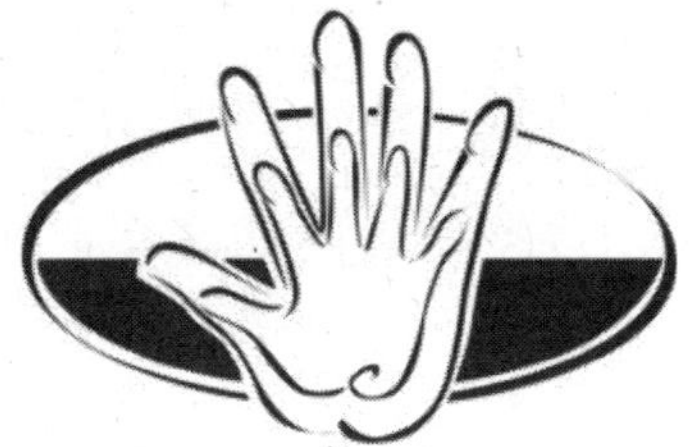

## Bruce Benko

2010
The ABC's Press
Houston, Texas

The ABC's Press
P.O. Box 19632
Houston, TX 77224-9632


ISBN Number: 978-0-9820278-8-2
Library of Congress Control Number: 2009903959


*Publisher's Cataloging-in-Publication data*

Benko, Bruce, 1966-
  The Gymnastics of Love & Discipline : A Parental Template
for Giving Children a Voice / Bruce Benko.
  p. cm.
  ISBN 978-0-9820278-8-2

1. Childrearing. 2. Parenting. 3. Preschool children—
Conduct of life. 4. Child development. I. Title.
HQ769 .B49 2009
649.1—dc22                                    2009903959


**www.CoachBruceBenko.com**

**www.TheGymnasticsOfLoveAndDiscipline.com**


Project Coordinator—Rita Mills
**www.bookconnectiononline.com**
Editorial Team
Faye Walker, Peggy Stautberg, Debbie Frontiera, Shirin Wright
Jacket Design & Line Art—Gladys Ramirez
Text Design —Rita Mills


The paper used in this publication meets the requirements of the American National Standard for Permanence of Paper for Printed Library Materials Z39.48-1984.

Printed in Canada

# Table of Contents

## To My Sister Kelly

Kelly showed me about life through tough love but also through example. She asked the right questions and always supported me with direction. She leads her life by being positive and making the hard choices (including being a vegetarian, seeing drug-, alcohol-, and tobacco-free, and choosing life as her high). In other words she doesn't just say it—she does it and does it with a kind heart. She showed me that life isn't about me, it's about others; but that I should not forget I have my opinion to guide me.

When I was younger, she always stood up for me and I knew it. She protected me with her words and she wouldn't let anyone do anything without a reason. She would have protected me until death and I knew it. I think that was the one thing that helped me the most: "I knew it." I knew if I needed someone I could trust and count on with 100% certainty it was Kelly.

As I became older, she continued to help me by making me look at myself honestly, and she did not accept anything less. This allowed me to keep learning and forced me to stop making bad decisions and to start thinking on a healthier level for myself. This I found to be very difficult. I didn't realize how "off" I was as a person until Kelly made me look at who I was. She made me see I wasn't being honest with myself and that helped me learn how to grow. By holding herself to a higher standard, she modeled what I needed to do so I could learn to do the same, and I believe that has allowed me to become a better person. So I say now: "I love you, Kelly, for being my Big Sister." You have really made a difference in my life, and I hope one day I can pay it forward.

———

# Acknowledgements

## To Dr. Kay Albrecht and Carla Gwinn

Dr. Kay Albrecht is the most brilliant woman I know when it comes to the teaching process. She set a precedent in Houston, Texas, by having her teachers stay with their children throughout the whole early childhood development period from birth through kindergarten. She had the foresight to understand that children would feel better and learn faster if their teachers didn't change every year. She also contributed to the development of the National Association of Education for Young Children's Early Childhood Program, an accreditation process I wholeheartedly believe in. She has written numerous books, including a curriculum for infants, toddlers, and preschoolers. She is an advocate for high quality early childhood education for every child.

I have had the privilege of working with her for fourteen years, and most of what I know I learned from Dr. Kay and from Carla Gwinn. They allowed me to teach my gymnastics/gross motor development program at their HeartsHome Early Learning Center because they saw how I was changing each child's life. They promoted my program so every parent would sign up, and a parent couldn't afford it, I always allowed the child to attend for free.

Carla Gwinn is absolutely the best teacher I have ever seen. I would sit in her classroom and just listen to what she would say. Through her actions I could see her brilliance shine.

I learned so much from watching these women in the classroom; I believe I am a shadow of what these women are. I took everything they said, melded it with my ideas, and formulated that material to my teaching style, which helped me become the coach I am today.

I still have ties with some of the children who attended school at HeartsHome, and I can honestly say that they are some of the most amazing young adults I have ever known. The way these women changed so many children's lives has always inspired me to have a gentle heart in my gymnastics classroom, but most of all to have a plan and stay consistent.

Dr. Kay and Carla Gwinn have also made me a better person! I would never have reached this level of understanding and foresight if it were not for their love of education and passion for children. These women are what every educator should strive to be. But most of all, I want to thank them for not giving up on their innovative ideas because, let me tell you, I know how *hard* it was to implement those ideas in the beginning.

I would also like to thank Brenda, Cheryl, Ellen, Linda, and Masami, teachers at HeartsHome, because I learned so much from them as well. Watching those teachers all these years also showed me how hard their jobs really are because I saw how serious they were about teaching.

One small example of this dedication is Masami. Here was an Asian man who could barely speak English; he began at HeartsHome working with infants. Now keep in mind he couldn't even communicate with them. But he was determined to be a teacher. I watched this young man grow into one of the most promising educators possible; it was amazing. He took those children from infancy to the age of six years and, let me tell you, he did a remarkable job. During this whole process, he found the time to finish his college education, learn the English language, and become a highly qualified teacher.

All of these teachers are brilliant and should be acknowledged for their great work with children. We all basically lived Dr. Kay's dream.

Lastly, I would like to thank them all for showing me what "use your words" means and how to apply it, for if it were not for them, I would never have been able to understand. So, Dr. Kay and Carla, I thank you again for giving me a voice so I can help others have theirs.

— · —

## Special Thanks

Mimi—You are my best friend for life. What is it—twenty-five years now? I will never forget your support and friendship through this whole process. Your faith in me made all the difference; I am looking forward to the next twenty-five years.

Dora Capello—The big things like life should come first, and there is a **great** possibility I would not be alive if it weren't for your kindness through my illness. As well as that, you are a friend for life and I thank you for allowing me to live in comfort while I wrote this book.

Mom—You have been a huge support factor for me. You allowed me to use you as a sounding board and it helped me mentally and emotionally. Your support cannot go without mention. It truly made all the difference. I am so happy this book has helped you become a better Mom. We are now on the same page.

Dad—I appreciate your willingness to open up more with me and to try to build a relationship now that we are older. Having you in my life again eases some of the pain in my heart. I hope we can continue to grow as father and son because the way I see it, you are worth it. I also want you to know I am proud of you. You and I have come a long way these past few years.

Kelly—I would also like to thank you for helping me digest Peggy's assessment as well as giving me ideas to write about. Because you taught with me, you saw firsthand what I did and really helped me recall information that directly pertained to this book. Your love for life helped me focus my thoughts so I could write them down (since I am not a writer). You are a huge part of why this book was written.

Chris Hiller—You were one of my mentors and I learned patience from you. Watching you teach children, I saw how important it was to pay attention to each child's feelings before mine. It was you who showed me a very important thing in life and that is to remember nothing gets accomplished if I get upset.

To all the teachers I worked with—A part of every one of you is in me. Each of you inspired me. I am a part of you all. Thank you for taking the time to answer all of my questions as well as for being the teachers you were. I can only hope one day the teachers in this world could receive more recognition for their work with children because I am only a shadow of who these people are.

Rita Mills—You did a great job with the layout of this book. Thank you for taking me by the hand and walking me through this whole process. The Book Connection is the reason this went so smoothly. Your direction and advice served me well. You always went over and beyond what you would normally do. Please remember you helped make this whole project really happen.

Peggy Stautberg—Thank you for taking my thirty-five manuscript pages and helping me turn them into a book. Your ability to take information out and keep its contents on track amazed me. You helped make all of our jobs much easier.

Faye Walker—Thank you for taking everyone's work and bringing it all together. I commend your ability to take Peggy's edits, and my words and make them flow with a clearer meaning. You are brilliant in what you do and are an extremely intelligent woman. I wish you success with your own writing career. Again Faye, you're the best.

Susan Schmidt (of www.ChildHelp.org)—Thank you so much for helping me with the references and websites. This material will give parents so much insight if they choose to seek out this information. You have done a wonderful service for all parents by giving me the direct studies that pertain to my philosophy.

Debbie Frontiera—Thank you for your help with the editing input as well as the research you did for me.

Sandy Lawrence—Your marketing team at Perceptive Marketing has a huge job ahead of it. I just want to thank you now for I can tell you will do a wonderful job. Your team is incredible and I have no doubt you will take me where I want to go.

Swaroop Dabhi—I want to thank you for helping me with the Teachers' Wish List.

Focus Group—Thank you, focus group that met at LaMadeleine's and gave me so much wonderful input on the cover as well as the artwork. I hope you like the new look. And, a special thanks to Jan Bethancourt, who came up with the title at the focus group.

Shirin Wright—Thank you for being the last pair of eyes that looked at the grammar aspect of this book. You were a blessing who came into the picture at the last minute, and did a wonderful job of finding little things that we had overlooked.

———•———

Bruce Benko provides us with a uniquely positive insight on love and discipline through this "template" on how to effectively raise productive and valued individuals. His understanding of how a child thinks and processes our words and behaviors is essential to becoming effective parents. I love how he helps us reduce our own anger during high stress times by helping us understand where our child is coming from, and as a result allows us to discipline in love and respect. Child abuse is rampant in our nation—five children die every day as a result of abuse or neglect . . . which is unacceptable. Most parents do not want to harm their child but discover that parenting can be a difficult task. Each of us has a responsibility to LEARN how to parent in the best possible way…with love and respect; understanding that at times our emotions get the better of us. This book resonates with love and respect— and provides a powerful guide and "how to" for parents across the nation on how to accomplish the most wonderful and most important jobs in a manner that will grow healthy, well-adjusted adults.

—**Susan L Schmidt MC NCC**
Director, www.ChildHelp.org
National Child Abuse Hotline

# Introduction

Are you frustrated because your child is out of control, talking back or *screaming* back or you can't seem to discipline him or her with words or spanks or even bribes? Are you losing control of your relationship with your child? I can show you how to get control back. If you are a frustrated parent who doesn't know what to do with your child, or if you feel you don't know how to discipline, I can give that control back to you with The Power.

The Power is not something I expected to find. I didn't even realize what it was until one day a parent asked me how it felt to be so comfortable around children and to know that if anything went wrong, I knew how to handle it correctly. At first, I wasn't even sure what she meant, but after our conversation was over, it hit me. She did not have the confidence or the communication skills to deal with her own child, and here I was, not even a parent, and could feel so comfortable about my interactions with any child. This is where I learned that most parents want to know how to be a better parent. This is where I learned I could help parents because I *do* know the way children think. I *do* have the answers to why children do some of the things they do. I've discovered that this technique of communication—the words I use when I talk to a child, the way I talk to a child, how I talk to a child, the respect I give to a child—gave me a way to deal with the children.

Having the ability to obtain and use this power will be a very comforting support for all parents. This power gave me peace of mind because I knew I was teaching the child in a healthy and safe way, and that allowed me to stay focused and calm in a potentially volatile environment. The Power allowed me to accomplish so much because

I was coming from a protective, not a punishing, place, and the children knew it.

The definition of The Power is being able to communicate with your child on their level, having the words and word patterns to calm them down, to de-escalate any situation, and to know that what you are doing is correct because it is helping your child. Once this power is obtained it will allow:

- Your child to tell you with their words what is going on in their minds…

- Which, in turn, will show you that your child does not understand about life and our adult concepts…

- And that will allow you to calm down and help you to correct their problems in a fair and reasonable way.

I would like to share with you what I have learned about children's behavior based upon my classroom experiences with about 10,000 children over the course of twenty-five years, and by having observed well over one hundred teachers in their classrooms. From these experiences, I've gotten positive results from the teaching and the communication methods that I developed.

I started a mobile gymnasium called Texas Tumblers™ in 1992. I have every piece of gymnastics equipment you can buy. This equipment was scaled down so that I could transport it in my van, then set it up at a school. At some schools, I could just leave it in place.

My non-competitive gymnastic/gross motor development program allows each child to learn at his or her own pace. Because I choose to be kind and patient, the children reward me by staying in my class for most of their childhood years. (In today's busy and over-scheduled world, this does not happen very often; children tend to go from being interested in something one day to being bored with it the next.) Few people are able to have this kind of long-term insight into how a child develops over the course of their childhood. I have been involved with the families as well as seen the children in their school environments and playing with their friends. Because my programs are intricately intertwined with schools, I have been involved with the children, their friends, their families, the teachers, and even the directors.

Because I use a mobile gymnasium, I move from school to school and have worked at some of the top private schools in Houston and Sugar Land, Texas, for twenty-two years. I have been privileged to work with over a hundred incredible teachers for most of their teaching careers. I sat in their classrooms, observed their teaching styles, watched the children's learning styles, and asked thousands of questions, which they kindly answered. I have also taught at nationally, and locally accredited schools.

I am the only one who has worked with *all* of these educators. No one has this information from my perspective—*because they never worked with one another*. I got to see them in action and was able to observe the workable methods they used with children. I modeled what they did and carefully and systematically applied it to my program.

Besides teaching children, I have talked about my theories and use of communication skills in open discussion with several groups of teachers to get their perspective as trained educators. In these discussions, I also learned that teachers really need support, and that a lot of parents are not doing enough to participate in their children's lives at school.

When you read this book, I think it is important to keep in mind that all of my theories are based upon my firsthand experiences with thousands of children. I have worked with children for all of my adult life, and I have learned many things about their behavior and the way they think. Many of the things I will share with you are things I learned from a child's perspective. I care about protecting children and the information in this book is intended to do just that.

I also used my own memories of how it was when I was a child, how I felt when things were done to me or how I felt about being a child. As an example, I was raised by parents who really didn't know how to be parents. They basically relied on their own history of how they were raised and left it at that. After writing this book, I have come to the conclusion that my parents had no idea what they were doing and in fact most of their efforts with me were harmful. As a child, I felt lost because my parents were not involved in my life, they did not ask the right questions, and I felt they did not help support my efforts to do well. Maybe that's why I am so protective of children and eager to give them a voice. The lack of parent participation and engagement in a child's life can be extremely harmful to a child.

In Part I—Communication, Why It Isn't Happening—I will impart the methods I used to get a better understanding of what is really going on in your child's mind, as well as the best way to get the best result. I will also give you the verbal tests that I did on children. These tests are meant for you to do with your child so you can see firsthand what your child may and may not understand.

I am blunt in my approach to educating you about what I have learned because that is the quickest. I will try to take you back to when you were a child so I can get you to start thinking like me. I will also break down what it means to be accountable and consistent as well as explain what trust, having patience, and giving support really mean. Remember that a parent is someone who is responsible and pays attention.

Another very important communication technique I want to show you is a method of speaking I learned from Dr. Kay Albrecht, Carla Gwinn and staff that I call "Word Patterns." These Word Patterns allow children to understand me and what I am asking for in a specific but kind way. These Word Patterns will be your tools to combat everything your child does and will work if you practice them. I know this because the eagerness and willingness I saw from some of the wildest children took my breath away. The ability for them to stay focused through my words, in my controlled environment made me start to think I had something special to help children. As I watched these children overcome fear and gain confidence through the words I used, I knew I'd found an amazing tool.

I eventually figured out why children listen to me and do as I ask: I'm protecting them by teaching them how to have a voice. I will not allow anything to happen to a child without giving the child a chance to protect himself. I start the sentence and they finish it, and that's my rule. Allowing children to say the words shows them how to protect themselves. What I do is give them the foundation and let them know it is important for them to say the words so they feel in control.

I will give you ideas about how to handle your child so you can gain back the control you may have lost by helping *them gain control* of their actions.

Most important, I will talk about "The Power" and what it means to obtain it through teaching rather than scolding.

In Part II, I will talk to you about your child's viewpoint, how he understands or doesn't understand your words and phrases, how he gets or doesn't get the discipline that you give. I will tell you when your child is scared and how to break them out of that blank stare, as well as what happens when you stop engaging in your child's life. I will tell you why I apologize to children as well as what I think happens in a child's mind when they say "I'm sorry." I would like to share with you what I do when a child breaks my rules or what I do in a difficult situation.

In Part III, I talk about teachers' wish lists (things they need from parents) which in turn would make their incredibly hard jobs a lot easier. Because I have had the privilege of working with hundreds of teachers, I asked them about their relationship with you and all of their answers concerned me enough to talk about it now. Here is what they said and why. I think it would be a good idea if you heard it from them.

Also in Part III, I talk about how important gross motor development is to a child and what happens mentally when they are *not* exposed to gymnastics or similar programs. I talk about something I believe and have been following for some twelve years. I call it "setting the mind" or "making a picture for the mind to remember." In this chapter, I discuss my belief that I have discovered something very important to every parent and explain why, when we become older we don't have rhythm, timing, tempo, coordination, and balance. Ever heard the saying "You are set in your ways"? Well, I am going to enlighten you as to why this could be happening!

My style of teaching brings together many different ways of thinking, old and new ideas, and real-life situations, making my method unique. Many educators, psychologists, and medical doctors who have written about child behavior agree with me. I sent my researchers out to discover books, articles, and websites that would make it easy for you to find the nitty-gritty (absolutely necessary) research that makes my work credible. Of course you want to know that the instructions I'm going to give you are respected and that the underlying ideas are supported by other professionals. I respect you for that! The end of Part III will lead you in that direction.

Giving your child a voice not only empowers children, it also teaches them it is okay to protect themselves. I teach them the correct way to handle situations and show them how to be in control when a parent is not around. Giving your child a voice will help them be unafraid and is the best thing parents can do for their children.

———•◆•———

# Foreword

Every parent has been there. Stumped. Stuck. Frustrated. Wondering what to do. Wondering how to get started. Wondering why. The book you are about to read will change all of that. It will give you a place to start, a way to get unstuck, great ideas about what to do and how to get started and, most important, an understanding of why.

How did Bruce Benko, gymnastic coach extraordinaire, figure it out? How did he come up with workable ideas that beg to be tried? The answer is simple—he watched, listened, and fit what he learned into his unique style of interacting with young children every day in his gymnastic classes. Practice made perfect—as he tried out his own synthesis of what he had learned, made in-course corrections, modified classroom teaching strategies, and learned from the uniqueness of the many children he was teaching. The result is altogether delightful and powerful and proves that great ideas can come from unlikely sources.

I met Bruce when I was on a journey of my own. I had spent my career in academia—working in laboratory settings with children under the age of eight. When a family move took me away from all of that to a place without a similar setting, I was forced to find my way in the real world. HeartsHome Early Learning Center was the result—and HeartsHome needed a gymnastics coach.

Bruce appeared; I liked his approach, his scope and sequence for motor learning, and he was flexible enough to move around to wherever we could find a place for him to teach—even if that meant going outside on the playgrounds. So, in the beginning, with my hands full running a school, keeping faculty and staff on task and happy, and collaborating with families in their children's educational lives, I was just glad to have filled the position.

Over time, that changed. As he taught, he learned from us and we learned from him. He watched talented and creative teachers at work teaching, borrowed ideas, molded them into his own, and applied them to his work with children. He loved the result and so did we.

There is much to be said for Bruce's enthusiasm. He had a smile on his face regardless of the challenges we faced at HeartsHome or any challenges he faced with our constant moving of his classroom and amending his class size. This attitude allowed us to work together for over fourteen years in enhancing the motor experiences available to enrolled children.

He is also generous. When financial challenges presented themselves, Bruce held steady to his goal—including children in motor experiences that were growth-producing and validating of the children who participated—regardless of their ability to pay.

Read his ideas. Try them out. The result will certainly be worth the time. And, it may result in a whole lot more than you expect. In fact, it may be enough to support you in giving your child a voice.


**—Kay Albrecht, Ph.D.**
Innovations in Early Childhood Education, Inc.

# *the* Gymnastics *of* Love & Discipline

# A Parental Checklist

These questions are meant to make you think, because I believe they should be on every parent's radar as a compass for parenting.

- Are you engaged in your child's life enough to see things from their perspective, so you can help them through love and respect?

- When your child accomplishes goals or overcomes fear, do you feel it was because you were supporting them by being engaged in their life?

- How are you rewarding their efforts and accomplishments? Can you see how those rewards are benefiting their life?

- How much time do you spend with your child when they are out of school? How are you helping prepare them for when they go back to school?

- Is your discipline plan and way of reasoning helping your child's life?

- Do you know when your child is afraid of you? Are your coping skills (dealing with your anger) showing in your relationship with your child?

- When your child upsets you do you realize they don't understand your reasoning? Are you being patient?

- What is your relationship like with your child right now? Who runs the household, you or they?

- Do both parents agree on the same discipline plan?

- Do you threaten, yell, or spank your child?

# PART I

## Communication, Why It Isn't Happening

# Navigating the Text
## Side Bars Explained

**Black Background** — Author is sharing his classroom experience

**Gray Background** — Author's affirmations based on a child's point of view on life and discipline

## Remember When?

Now in the next chapters, I want to relate to you as a person who was once a child and talk about how the world has changed since we were children. I also want to let you know that much of the information we learned when we were children was wrong, and how that translates into how we think today, so that you can develop a better understanding of what parenting should be all about.

We were not able to begin any kind of school until we were five years old. Now in the twenty-first century, you can bring your infant to a day care center and he or she will be taken care of. That was unheard of when we were children. Also we did not have much modern technology to distract us, only TV or radio.

The pace of the world has changed and children are being left behind. In today's world, both parents have to work in order to raise a family, which in turn leaves the child behind. Your children spend more time at school each year than they do with you, and because of this, many parents expect our educators to discipline children or teach them how to behave. This puts the teacher in a difficult position. A teacher's job is to inspire and teach, so please don't get it confused with raising your child

> **Learning to accept that we need to change how we talk to our children is a must.**

for you, which is discipline or correcting bad behavior. I find the less time a parent spends with his or her child, the more time that child spends trying to find attention and acceptance through someone else. Children are so smart in today's world because they start learning so much earlier than we did, and because of this, we expect children to understand things they can't.

Just remember that a lot of the things we learned when we were children are not true and are not acceptable in today's world. For example, almost every history book we learned from is no longer in publication because we have learned we were wrong about a lot of the information. New books had to be written. We no longer exercise the way we used to because we have now found that some methods or positions actually put more stress on parts of the body, which could increase injuries. We used to think infants and toddlers were not capable of learning much until they got older, and now we have proven they can. I figure most things in life we learned when we were children were just guesses and now we are finding out, because of technology and time, that we guessed wrong. Learning to accept that we need to change how we talk to our children is a must.

## It Helps Me to Think Back to When I Was a Child

I always wondered why I never had a voice, why my parents always told me what to do with no explanation ("Because I told you so!"), why I was just expected to do. When my father yelled or when he spanked me, I only got mad at him for spanking me, which made me scared of him most of my life regardless of how many times he may have told me he was "doing this for my best interest" or that he was showing me he cared. I never got that. I remember feeling completely lost as a child and the only thing that brought me out of it was growing up.

I also remember wishing someone would listen to me, or wondering why it always had to be like that, or wishing they would stop doing that. As a child, I felt useless because of the way my father always talked down to me. I always felt confused, which made me learn out of fear. It always seemed my mistakes were bigger than what I had accomplished. I mostly felt things were backward, and that made it hard for me to know right from wrong or good from bad. Keeping me scared and confused made me gullible, and I didn't like it. I knew something was wrong, but I was too young to figure it out. Most of the time, I just did what everyone said, even if I didn't agree. As children, we think it is us that's causing all the problems because we get blamed for most everything when, in fact, it's the adults that are the problem.

**Some questions to think about:**

- What was your relationship like with your parents when you were a child?
- What style of discipline did your parents use? How did that make you feel?
- What types of childhood experiences will you want to pass along to your child?
- What types of childhood experiences will you want or not want him to have?
- What behavior patterns did your parents use that you want to use with your own children?
- What behavior patterns do you want to avoid?

## Reality Check

Remember, parents: it all starts with you. You have to want to change so you can teach your child. I can tell you the answer, but that does not mean you will change. Change, for most people is extremely hard. I know this way of thinking worked for me and even though it was hard to learn, it is simple to apply, so keep that in mind.

It is important for you to commit to what I am saying: understand that you must change how you use language with your child. Language must be used to gain your child's trust. I will continually ask you either to calm down or tell you not to get upset. Anger, frustration, indecision, and guessing is what has gotten you to where you are now, so you have to try something else. It is hard to trust me, but I promise this change will work. Once you figure out your new verbal method and apply it, everything else becomes much easier. I also want to let you know up front that this method will make you engage in your child's life and will make you be held accountable for everything you do that in turn forces your children to be held accountable for everything they do. It's good to let your children know when you make mistakes. Telling them you were wrong goes a long way in helping your child understand no one is perfect. We all make mistakes and it is hard to learn without making them. I believe some families have good or great relationships mainly because they have good or great communication skills with one other as well as the ability to forgive one another.

Parents start guessing because they are rushed for time.

Learning how to listen is just as important as speaking. Learning to listen is how I will get you to understand that anger and frustration are self-inflicted. For example, just asking your child how he or she is doing is not enough. You must ask, "What?" and "Why?"—not "What are you doing?" or "Why did you do it?". Ask "What is my child trying to say?" and "Why is she saying it?" By figuring out what the child was trying to say, I came to a lot of my conclusions as well as why they were saying it. Learning to look at children as children also helps. Engaging your child with the proper words and phrases will help you learn about them. I find most parents have lost the concept of raising children because of the pressures the world brings. Also, a lot of single parents are raising their children on their own.

When you begin to understand how children really think, you can stop guessing. As you learn how to combat their tests and trials (because children will test you and test you and test you), you will remember that you're the parent and they are the child. I see a lot of moms and dads so overwhelmed that it almost seems they are their child's friend simply because they don't know what else to do. As this process starts, you will see how your child changes as he begins to trust you and not fear you. Once your child trusts you, an amazing thing will happen. They will stop testing so much and, best of all, their behavior becomes better because they now know you're serious and committed. They will start to predict your actions. As a parent, you want your child to predict your actions because that shows you are consistent and engaged. A lot of the word patterns we will use will help you and your child understand each another so you can both calm down.

Finally, this process will show you that your child doesn't understand adult concepts, reasoning, or the big picture. Therefore, you need to stop thinking they do and realize your child is a child and they need your love and understanding, not anger, frustration, hostility, or threats. Understanding that your child doesn't understand the word "why" (when you ask them why) will also help you get a better understanding of your children.

I also think it is important you realize I haven't used the word "punishment" and that is because we are talking about "communication." I will get to punishment (discipline or what I call "child's currency") later. Let's first concentrate on communication.

———

## Your Child Is Not Your Friend

I understand why you try to be your child's friend, but if you only get one thing from this book let it be—that is not an option! These next sections are about how your efforts to be your child's "friend" can actually harm your child if you are not careful. If you look up the word "friendship" you will see the word "parenting" is nowhere to be found. If you are your child's friend or are trying to be because you don't know what else to do, then just realize your child knows they are the one in control of the household and won't give up that control easily. I wrote this book so that you have a better understanding of the way children think and what they need from you. I will be giving you numerous choices of how to deal with your children when you feel they are out of control. If you follow my word patterns plus stay consistent, you will become a better parent and realize parenting has nothing to do with friendship. Children need someone to be the parent, the one they can count on and, most of all, *learn* from. From a child's point of view, a parent is someone who shows the child about life, helps them to understand about himself, and teaches them right from wrong.

The parent has to be the bad guy sometimes. It comes with the territory. Parenting is taking responsibility for your children and being held accountable for their actions. It's serious work and should be taken seriously. Being your child's friend will upset almost every value you could possibly teach them because you're not starting off with the mindset of a parent. A parent should be very protective and should think about the child first. A parent should be someone who loves and cares for the child, offering guidelines and rules they must follow without fear. But most of all a parent should be fair. If you are fair, your child will pick up on it and respect you for it. Don't ever forget, when it comes to your children, they are very smart about what they want and need and if you are fair, they will reward you by listening to your words.

## Stop Guessing When It Comes to Your Child

Parents start guessing because they are rushed for time. Remember when I said adults need to stop thinking they know what their child is thinking? For example: Let's say your child walks up to you and hands you a piece of artwork and you say, "Oh, how nice," "Pretty," "Thank you," or something like that. Wrong. Wrong. Wrong. Never guess. Your child spent all this energy doing this piece of art and when they give it to you, you guessed what it was and were wrong. I have seen so many parents do just this and later the child walks up to me and says it was really a dragon or cat or bird or whatever—just not what you guessed. See how this can disrupt their sense of values? Plus, by guessing, you hurt your child's feelings. What you should say is, "What is it?" Then after the description you could say things like, "Why did you draw that?" or "Why did you choose the color?" or "I like that color," or "Do you like drawing?" or so many inquiring or descriptive comments.

Do you see how if you ask your child about their work or actions it takes the guesswork out of it? Children need adults to inquire about the things they do at school and ask questions about the things the child liked or disliked instead of just accepting them at face value. Children know when you pay attention and when you don't. When it comes to things about them, children are masters of control and will very nearly lay down their lives in order to get control and keep it. If you stop guessing when it comes to your children, they will stop fighting you for control.

They will know who is in control and not have to guess or, better yet, it probably won't ever come up because children would rather be led than have to demand.

## It's Not About You or Your Feelings!

Let me tell you how I give up my will. I can do this because I have a word plan when a child does something right or wrong. You will learn it's not about you; it's how you choose to handle it with your words. Don't forget the early sections are only meant to get you thinking, and now I will give you an idea of how to handle situations.

In order for this communication technique to work, you have to be willing to give up your will. That means when your child makes you, mad or upset, you have to be willing to trust that yelling or hitting doesn't work. And if you truly believe that, then you must trust what I'm going to say really is how your child feels and thinks.

As soon as you scare or hurt your child, your child gets upset at you or just plain mad. (It is a normal defense mechanism for all children.) Your child is not thinking they deserve their punishment because they don't think they did anything wrong. The only thing that crosses their mind is you are scaring them or hurting them and their defense is to get mad at you. Thus the teenager says, "I hate you" or "That's not fair"; the toddler hits you or says, "No"; and the preschooler shrugs her shoulders and says, "I don't know," or gives you a blank stare. That blank stare is telling you "I'm scared."

In my many years of working with children, I have tested this issue and the only way I get a positive result is to first apologize for my actions. Then I proceed to tell them I didn't mean to scare them or hurt their feelings, but their bodies or actions scared me so I didn't have a choice. (This apology is huge. It must be done for this to work. It will help your child calm down and listen. I will get further into this in an upcoming chapter.)

Children understand my fear because they fear things, too. Then I tell them why I chose to respond the way I did. (I believe if you use my word patterns correctly, you can talk about other people's feelings. This is an example of a word pattern I would use to explain that people have feelings: "You hurt my feelings.") Because hitting or yelling doesn't work, I ask you to try using my word patterns and see for yourself. Talk with your child as you would to any other person's child. Most of the time children are not trying to be mischievous; they are just curious and like to test how you will react or to see if you're paying attention.

I believe consistency in your behavior is essential in raising a child; otherwise, you will have behavioral problems like noncompliance, whining, and obstruction. Not only do children like being told what's going on and why rather than being dragged around, they also will be more interested in complying if they can rely on your consistency. I have also found that giving up my will doesn't allow me to get so upset at what a child does; rather, it allows me to communicate and teach a child just by showing it's not about me or my feelings. This alone has helped me to calm down, and to handle each situation with a different attitude because I now know what is really going on in a child's mind.

Even though your child's discipline is not about you or your feelings, your child is always measuring you and your feelings, often without your knowing it. I find in my play arena that children mimic parental behavior, especially in the anger department. When a child is in the play arena and another child upsets them, they treat that child in the way they are treated by you. If you're aggressive, they are, and if you're not, they're not.

I understand children learn some through violent cartoons or when they role-play, but I also believe a lot of your personality traits come out in your children when they are in their play arena.

———

## Children Are Smart
## When It Comes to What They Want

Everyone in the family must be on the same page. This is all about respect and trust! Most children, from an early age, figure out how to get what they want when they want it by throwing a temper tantrum, screaming out loud, or whining, and if that doesn't work then they can always count on either Mom or Dad stepping up to the plate. If both parents don't agree on a discipline plan, the children will pick up on this. They will test the weaker parent until he or she doesn't know what else to do but give the screaming child what he wants.

When children get to this stage, it tells me your child has completely lost respect for you and you are no longer in control. Your child is now running the household because there is no consistency when it comes to your words or discipline. All of these issues stem from the lack of respect and trust. Yes, respect and trust. It has nothing to do with discipline. Respect and trust are the way children learn boundaries. If a child trusts you have their best interest in mind and they respect you for it, they will not test. Only try. Trying and experimenting are ways children learn. You can't take that away. If a child trusts the outcome will be the same every time, testing will not be an issue. If they truly trust, then they will start talking to you more and asking permission. Yes, permission. Children have a tendency to do unto others as is done unto them. Children will mimic bad behavior and when they figure out that good behavior is better than bad behavior, you will have an unbelievably happy child.

Your children are punished by others when you are not doing your job. I find children who are "bad" or misbehave are treated differently than the children who listen and pay attention. See how the lack on your part could cause other people to be mean to your child just because you didn't teach them how to have respect for others. It is important for parents to know their child suffers every time they fail to teach them something about life.

## Consistency and Accountability

Repeating yourself shows consistency, and leading by example shows accountability!

> **I feel badly let down when promises are broken.**
>
> I find the worst thing I can do is tell a child I am going to do something and not follow through. When this happens, children get their feelings hurt, and most of the time, they think they did something wrong. That is why I never make rash promises. I also get the feeling that when I let a child down they get disappointed and slowly stop trusting me; or worse, when I do make a promise they are less likely to believe or trust me.

Children's minds hunger for consistency and accountability. Just so you know, the word consistency comes from the word "constancy," meaning having the ability to maintain a particular standard or repeat a particular task with minimal variation. All children are very smart when it comes to them and what they want and what they want is for you to be consistent and fair. When they get this, I find children are very consistent themselves, which makes everyone's job easier. I have been so successful because the children keep hearing me say and do the same thing every time a child acts in a certain way. I find the more I repeat the same behavior, the more it works for the child.

You can see that consistency helps children start to predict your moves so they will respect and trust your choices. Consistency in your life is how your child learns there is an order to things, which makes them feel safer. The safer your child feels and the more he trusts you, the more he will tell you when you ask.

Accountability ties everything together because it makes us responsible for our actions. The definition of accountability is to be responsible to somebody or for something. (This is why I tell children they are scaring me. It's because I am responsible for their actions while they are with me.) As a parent, you can teach your child that there are consequences for their choices and actions. First, being able to tell our children we were wrong; and why, shows them it is okay to make certain mistakes. Second, when we are held accountable for our actions, we can explain right from wrong to our children. Many parents scold their children for doing things that the parents do themselves. We must lead by example because expecting children to know better is the first mistake. Children learn right from wrong and when you are a parent who does not accept his or her mistakes, children don't just know it, they feel it.

*Keep me from forming bad habits (behavior that is not normal: flinching, mimicking, lying, and so on). I have to rely on you to detect them in my early stages.*

If you let a child form bad habits, it's harder for you to break them later on. Children don't understand what "bad habits" are. When they see someone else do it, they don't know they're not supposed to do it until they've tried it. Sometimes a child may experiment with a behavior to see what kind of response he'll get. Don't jump to conclusions, but if it becomes a habit, immediately speak to your child about why his behavior is not socially acceptable.

Remember, children are visual learners.

Please remember this: my hope in writing this book is to get you to understand that your child doesn't understand you and that repeating your behavior shows consistency. You should teach with a soft heart and not after the fact. So my advice to you is, lead by example and take responsibility for your child's actions.

## Trust



Just because you say, "I love you" doesn't mean your children trust it.

Trust is another essential when raising a child. If children trust you're looking out for their best interest, they will become proud of their decisions and start to learn how to be held accountable for their actions. If your child can trust with 100% certainty what you're going to do, if your child truly trusts you have her best interest in mind, and are not condemning her when she makes a wrong choice, she will stop testing. But if a child can't trust what you're going to do, he feels like he has no boundaries and will test you. In this case, you give him no sense of balance and he may become very emotional. If a child can trust you are not going to freak out either way and there will be fair consequences, most children won't even consider the bad choice because children mainly aim to please. They need to trust we love and support them no matter what they do, but they must not forget that consequences follow actions.

## Patience

I'm not talking about having patience when your child is doing right or you are just showing patience as a normal parent should. I'm talking about having patience when you don't want to.

Patience is how parents  learn to take their time so children can have time to think, which in turn allows children to learn and apply that learning to their lives in a kind way. The main reason children get upset is because you are not being patient, which means having the ability to endure waiting, delay, or provocation without becoming annoyed or upset or to stay calm when faced with difficulties. Patience is having enough love for your child that you allow them to learn at their own pace. Children do not learn faster if you rush them nor do they respond according to what you think they should be able to do. Children need to be on children-time, not adult-time.

If your children have anger problems, it's because you are not showing patience so they have no other choice but to rebel. They are angry and don't know how to defend themselves. Parents, your children are not out to hurt your feelings or destroy your day. If we can just learn children don't have the capability to understand their actions, then we can finally understand the way we discipline our children is not working. If you are patient when your child makes a mistake or does something wrong, he will reward you by listening to your words.

Example: Despite my long years of working with children, I too sometimes find myself getting angry with students; in every situation I find if I show love first, the child responds and I get a better

*It upsets my sense of values when you make me feel my mistakes are a big deal. Then I feel sorry for myself.*

A mistake is just a mistake, nothing more.  Do not place too high a value on mistakes.

Mistakes are how  we all learn and  are a part of life. When a child makes a mistake, don't treat it too harshly. Look at it as an opportunity to help and teach, to show your child how patient and willing you are to help. This is a great time to show your child you can be calm, but you don't have to be soft. Use child's currency. Just remember, when your child makes a mistake, this is a great time for you to correct the problem and bond  with  your child.

result. Children don't know how *not* to respond to love because that's what they always want and when they get it they know it. When a child hurts my feelings and does something wrong, my first question is always, "Do you need a hug?" Yes, a hug, because that way, the child knows right from the start he's not in trouble. That allows me to talk to the child so we can discuss their actions. When a child doesn't fear you, they will talk to you.

There is a reason I do not have the same behavioral problem that parents face and it's because I can see the outcome before it happens. I have the foresight through trial and error of how a child thinks and that makes me handle behavioral problems through teaching rather than scolding. It's as if I have a greater clarity of sight. Because of this sight, I have a choice to control the outcome before it even happens. I know if I handle the situation recklessly—acting impatiently or aggressively; not being fair; making children do things they're scared or unwilling to do—they will fight me and will remember how I treated them. Then I no longer have the child's respect or trust and they are learning out of fear. Knowing this, I keep from making little mistakes that I know will create a long-lasting domino effect. If you start thinking like me you'll be able to stop your children from repeating the same behavior. Showing respect, giving trust, and having foresight allows me to calm down and again realize if I handle things incorrectly with a child they will continue to repeat behavior I am asking them to stop. I know children do not understand my adult way of thinking. Please understand that's why the behavior problems keep happening with you and that's why they don't with me. This is the reward I get for everything I do with children. This can be your reward, too.

Discussing punishment with your child is the correct way to show patience (see Part II, Chapter 6). Even at age two and a half, children understand this concept when done right. They may not like it, but they learn in time that you will make them be held accountable and through patience this can be done without yelling or spanking. I know it's hard, but when you get the result you are looking for it will be worth it, trust me. Just remember there is always another way; you just have to keep trying, and I will keep giving you ideas.

## The All-Important "Why"

In this section you will learn how important this question "why" is. Almost everything I do is based on the reason "why." For me this is how I maintain order within myself because I always ask myself, "Why am I doing this?"

Children like to know "why." It makes them feel like they know what's going on or what's getting ready to happen. Using the phrase "Because I told you so" is not acceptable. This actually hurts the child's feelings and upsets their ability to ask questions. Children need parents to take the time to explain to them what's going on in the world and why. There's an important reason for this: talking to your children this way helps them learn to judge for themselves, and, when done correctly gives your child the ability to make sound decisions.

"Why" must be answered. This will also slow the testing issue and should make you feel good that your child is asking you questions. "Why" is another way of showing your child how to communicate with you, and it also shows the child they can trust and ask you questions without there being a punishment or a consequence for asking. "Why" is one of the safest ways to teach your child and it can be fun when done right. So please take the time to answer "Why." It will make a difference.

Many times I see parents not taking the time to explain "why" and in return children just don't get what you mean. In turn you feel like your child keeps testing you but if you follow the Power method, you address each issue *the same way every time*. Confronting your child's behavior is crucial to their understanding and if done correctly you will see your child blossom because they know what is expected and will not test so much. This will take a while but is worth it. I have discovered children pick up on confrontations. All my children know if they do something right or wrong there will be a confrontation and they like it. It makes them feel safe because they know I will praise them and protect them with their words and mine.

## Now *Your* Why

When you ask "why?" your child most likely gives you a blank stare. Have you ever noticed when you ask your child a simple question like "Why did you do that?" they can't answer the question or, better yet, they repeat an answer in a question. For example, in my class children learn about heights for safety reasons. Some children test this issue and when they do, I tell them, "That was too high to jump," and "You scared me," and "Please don't do it again." Then I ask the magic question: "Do you know why?" Their reply is always "It was too high" and not the correct answer, "Because I could hurt my body." Even when I try to coach them by saying, "You must not do that because you will hurt yourself," they never get it. They just keep repeating "too high" or "not to do that," never the correct answer of "I can hurt my body." In other words, they don't understand the reasoning; they're just repeating my words. When you as a parent understand this simple concept, you will see how little your children understand our adult world. A child will not answer if he or she is scared. They will lie or give you a blank stare. If you want your child to understand you, you can't scare them. You have to be patient when you ask "why?"

## Leaving Your Child at the Classroom

If parents only knew what happens when they leave! I have said at least a thousand times, "If you would just leave, your child would stop crying." Your children cry because they don't understand your needs and the responsibilities of having to go to work to make money to support the family. Please understand when you say, "Mommy has to go to work now," or "Daddy has to get money so we can go on vacation," or "You have to go to school," your child doesn't understand "Mom has to go to work"; he's just mimicking your answers. He doesn't understand and he isn't learning. I do understand it is hard for you to leave your screaming child, but if you would take the time *before you are in this situation* to talk about schedules, having to work, picking them up, and so on, it would help them in the long term. Parents, please don't say, "I told my child I have to go to work," or "I told them I will pick them up." This communication that I am talking about must be done *at home* when you are *not leaving*.

It's best if you talk to your children when you are all at home, just talking, preparing them for the coming week. They can't take in the reasons when you are in the car on the way to school. They need time to think about everything you've told them. Telling a child beforehand through role-playing, and letting them ask questions about why you have to leave and answering as well as you can *at their level of understanding* will help them cope. Then they can change their behavior as you give them the answers. Asking your child if they know why you are doing something before it has to be done is a huge step toward your child's understanding. For example, ask your child if he knows why you leave him at Coach Bruce's before he goes to school, and he will start to understand why you must leave. You have to remind them constantly in their daily lives that there are times when you have to leave, and you can do this by asking them questions to see if they know why you are leaving. Even if they are still having a hard time understanding, at least you know you always give them the correct answer to the question of why you have to leave.

Just seeing this situation from a different point of view does help sometimes. Adults think it's not such a big deal, but being left is

> ***I love experimenting. I couldn't get on without it, so please put up with it.***
>
> There is a difference between a child experimenting and a child misbehaving. The difference is the child is interested in what they are doing and interested in my reaction rather than being scared of getting into trouble. When a child experiments you can usually tell by the expression they have on their face and the way they react to you when you question what they are doing. I find experimenting is testing to see if I'm paying attention, or trying to see if they like something, or following what someone else did. Experimenting is not misbehaving and, in my opinion, should not be punished. This is how all children learn. You should talk about the experience with your child.

traumatic for your child. All I am trying to do is show you how your child might feel and give you examples of how I came up with some solutions.

Here is an example of what I am talking about.

Being late is a major reason children don't like being left. Children have a time schedule for everything except family, and when children are late, they know it because a teacher/coach will tell them. It's the way the world works, not the way your schedule runs. Being late for school or an activity upsets your child's whole day and it makes them feel like they did something wrong. Let's say that 9 a.m. is Group Time, one of your child's favorite parts of their morning, and they are missing it. They know by your reactions they're late; it now becomes a huge issue and all this could have been avoided if you were on time. This even includes parents who decide to take the morning off to hang out with their child and bring them in later. I suggest you clear it with your child first because, like I said, there might be a part of class they don't want to miss.

Most of the time the child is not crying because you're leaving; it is the way you are leaving. The lack of communication and reassurance scares them that you're not coming back. I know this because I see how the child acts when you leave and how long it takes for them to calm down and join the group. I started to notice that the child would re-group quickly because they didn't want to miss out on what was going on. Children are extremely aware of their world, and you need to remember that to a child life is all about them.

Now for the child that is just crying because you are leaving, please, once you arrive at the school, say your goodbyes, remind them that you have already talked about this, and you will be back to pick them up, and leave. Remember, one last hug or kiss is always nice.

I just want you to see it from a child's perspective so you can have a better understanding of why your child acts the way she does. I also hope this better equips you so you can handle the situation correctly by taking the time at the right time to make it work.

---

# Your Will Is Not Support

I believe getting correct support from parents is crucial to your child's social development. I believe it is the reason we as adults look back on our lives wanting to change our children's future. When I hear a parent say, "I want my child to have it better than I did," I believe what they are really saying is, "I will treat my child better than my parents treated me."

I believe we think this because, outside of money, the only thing we can change is how we treat our children. But we have only our experiences to draw on and, in today's world, that is not enough. I have learned the only way to learn how to treat our children better is to educate ourselves as much as we can and to have an open mind because no one person can do it all right all the time.

The definition of support is to give assistance or comfort to somebody in difficulty or distress. Support is about showing children your approval of what they're doing. In this chapter, you will learn how the right kind of support can be a tricky thing. You will learn the lack of support can lead to bad people taking advantage of your child. Plus, you will learn what correct support is so you can help your child when they ask for it.

Here are some phrases you can start using as encouragement:

1. Keep up the good work!
2. You can do it!
3. I am proud of you!
4. Stay focused.

I believe if you are not supporting your child through encouragement, you are placing your values and beliefs on to the child, and that is just not right. Support is not about you; it's about encouraging a child to follow his interests. Encouragement is letting them ask you for help by letting them be the ones in control. Take things from their lead. Only give them your opinion if they ask for it and try to stay out of their way (as long as it is in a controlled environment).

However, there is nothing wrong with asking questions. Questions are great and highly recommended. Asking questions is how we should protect our children. There is nothing wrong with your being protective, but make sure there is a place for it before you get too involved. Give your child the benefit of the doubt and ask questions if you are concerned. Show them support by trusting them, by trusting that they can make the right decision.

However, sometimes if you are not giving your child the right support, you could actually be hurting them. We have all seen the overbearing parent, the parent who is always helping too much. They are not helping their child. They are actually being intimidating and demanding and we all have learned through time these behaviors are harmful. So please make sure you are not that parent.

I can speak about this now. I felt my father's efforts to support or help me weren't there—all because I didn't understand his intentions nor his way of thinking. I also found that it made me want to please other people, and I have discovered that isn't a very good thing. When you are



If you are wishy-washy, your children will pick up on it and start to become very emotional (whiny). They will test you because they don't know where their, and your, boundaries are. Children rely on you for consistency in your behavior so they can learn from you. When you are firm with your children, they know their boundaries and feel reassured. They know that you are serious.

a child and have been programmed to please others, people take advantage of you. People always took advantage of my kindness.

Here is a list of things I believe happened to me because I did not get the correct parental support through encouragement; rather, I was told how and what to do.

1.  If there was something I was doing that I liked or was good at I always wondered why I didn't get the support I saw other children getting from their parents; that rejection or lack, in turn, made my heart sad, even lonely at times.

2.  The lack of encouragement made me feel like my best was not good enough.

3.  My father's dismissal of or refusal to acknowledge my actions made me feel like I was not doing most things right. That made me question myself a lot, and kept me confused and scared.

4.  Not getting a lot of encouragement made me feel I was always following when I really wanted to lead as well.

5.  Because my parents were not involved, I felt they did not care what I did.

6.  Sometimes I felt things were harder to accomplish than they actually were. It made me feel I was fighting inside myself with my parents because I was too scared or didn't trust them enough to tell them anything.

7.  I felt unwanted even though I was told I was loved. And that made me not believe anything they said because I didn't trust them in the first place.

## Engage in Your Child's Life

Your child is harmed when you don't give the correct support through encouragement as well as engagement in your child's daily life. If you look back to when you did not get the right support and engagement, you may still feel that pain to this day.

Now if support is not given, it can scare a child into lying and feeling sorry for themselves as well as keeping them from being engaged by you. This lack of engagement disrupts the whole flow of the child because the child no longer has any guidance from you when they become interested in something. What happens now is they start to lose confidence in your support because the only engagement they are getting is from an outside source.

I call it protection mode when this happens and your child's behavior changes. This basically means your child is now looking and longing for anyone to show them some kind of support, encouragement, and/or direction. (That is why kids sometimes copy others.) This is when your children are in real trouble: bad adults are able to take advantage of children by pretending to offer support and encouragement. Some children will become people-pleasers and will do anything to get that much-needed support.

Support is essential because that is how you show your child you are interested in what they are doing. When you engage in what they are doing, you show them direction and that you care. If we show support instead of frustration or anger, children learn mistakes are not sins—through trial and error is how we all learn. Support is what we all long for, so when it is given with love and understanding, children can truly grow in their own way and not be forced to be subservient. When we support our children, it teaches them that they can trust us without fear of punishment and that no one is perfect.

I hear so many times that parents would die for their children. Yet I find the seem unwilling to take the time to figure out that children don't understand certain things and only need support, encouragement, and direction through engagement; not yelling, threatening or spanking.

We live in such a fast-paced world, not made any easier by technology, that we need to slow back down and realize we are leaving our children behind. In order to give support, you have to give the time for it to work. You have to be there.

The bottom line is that everything a parent does with a child affects them later in life. Just remember—when your child is playing a sport or involved in dance, music, or theater, as soon as you tell a child what to do without their permission, you're no longer giving support. You are now telling them how to be.

## Helping Too Much Gives Me a Different Result

In my structured class the less I help a student after they have learned the skill, the faster the child learns. I found the more I help, the more the children asked for help when they did not need it, or expected me to help when they could do it on their own. I discover-ed the more I encouraged the children, as long as they felt safe, the more likely they were to try something on their own. I find outside the classroom, children need to learn in their own time in their own way. The only way to do this is for them to do it by



Children are constantly looking for attention and they get this through asking questions. Questions are how humans learn and build our brains, but more important, children find out how interested you are in them by the way you answer their questions.

Because I love all the children, their questions are important to me. And I want each child to know that by always answering them and allowing them to continue to ask their questions. I do this because I want to teach them to ask questions and to let them know that questions are how we find out the right and wrong answers. Children get disappointed easily. And if you leave it up to someone else to answer your child's questions, they may not get the answers you would give. So please take the time to answer their questions.

themselves after they initially learn a skill. Children start to build a fear barrier at an early age because everything is so hard and new.



When children are young, they hurt themselves quite often, which will create fear. There are a lot of children who are fearless until they break a bone or get hurt—then it ends. Once a child is about two years old, they should start some kind of age-appropriate developmental gross motor program like noncompetitive gymnastics to allow them to learn about their body and how it works in a correct but safe and monitored place. I say this because during my years of teaching I have watched thousands of children overcome their fears and gain confidence and self-esteem in my program with just the words I used and a lot of encouragement. Hearing a child say at an early age "I did it" with a big smile on their face is priceless. Plus, I have noticed children who learn about their body and how it works will do better in everything they try because they have the confidence to do it.

Confidence gives them the opportunity to learn how to play with other children without hurting them or getting hurt. Having the will to play because they can is a great way for children to learn how to play. I show them how to play, which gives them the concept and the rest is up to them. They get to decide if they want to do it or not. Through trust, support and encouragement I have noticed children will try, but most of all, it gives them the chance to conquer their fears on their own.

For your information, I believe parents who help too much disrupt this concept and actually slow down their child's learning process. All I know for sure is the more I help physically, the less the child learns about why they should do it on their own and, they also lose the feeling of pride that results when they do.

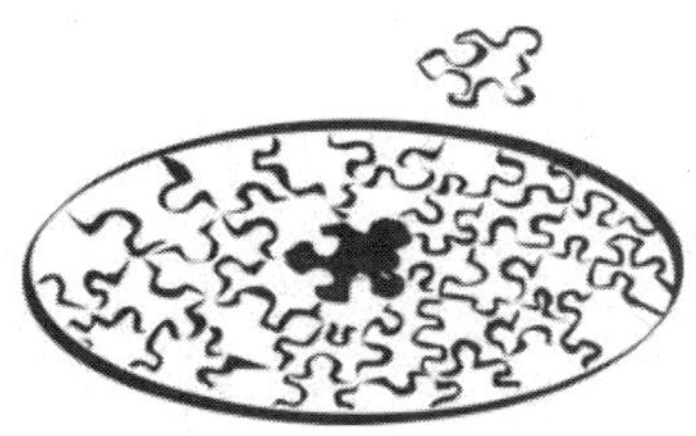

## Putting It All Together

Parents, I know you are trying. Our generation wasn't raised to deal with a twenty-first-century child. We were taught to listen and do. We weren't taught to ask a lot of questions about the world and our place in it. The world keeps changing and we keep obtaining information, but when it comes to raising children, we are always behind.

Nowadays, children have learned to mimic adult behavior so well that adults are confused into thinking children understand adult concepts when they don't. I also believe you're confused because you think they are so much smarter than you were. Children are children and need to be treated like children. They only have you to count on and most parents aren't doing a very good job, especially the parent who always gives an excuse for his or her actions: "I was too busy." "I was in a hurry." "I was running late." "I was . . . ."

Technology allows us to "have it now" and sometimes parents take advantage of that by saying to themselves, "I can always buy something for my child to make up for my missing the game" or something to that effect. But that is the problem.

I know when we treat children wrong, their personalities shut down and they become scared and submissive. That caused me to find a way that works for the child first, then for me. Children need to trust that we are not selfish and are willing to put our lives on hold to help them grow. Children in the twenty-first century may appear smarter than we were due to technology and early enrollment in schools, but don't let that confuse you. They are still children.

All I know for sure is if we don't raise our children in a different way, we're hurting them, not helping them.

Now what I would like to do in Part II is put you back in what I call "new school." It all starts by holding your children to a higher standard, by your leading by example, by holding children accountable. I did these things with my students and they *liked* it. I held each child accountable for their actions because I was held accountable for my actions first, and they showed me a lot of respect by listening to my words and doing as I asked.

---

**Some questions to think about:**

- Did you feel listened to as a child? Did your words matter to the important adults in your life? How so?
- What kinds of communication skills did your parents use with you? Looking back on it, how does that affect you today?
- What types of communication skills are you teaching your child today? Do you think they understand what you are trying to tell/teach them?
- What message do you want to send to your children with your communication skills of today? Do you think that message is being heard?
- What communication skills do you want to pass on to your child?
- What communication skills do you want to avoid and are you avoiding them?

# PART II

## The Power

## What Is The Power?

How do I get my child to listen to me? How do I get my child to do what I ask, when I ask them to do it? How do I calm down so I can handle my child's mistakes correctly? These are questions every parent asks himself or herself. These are questions teachers and coaches and art and dance instructors ask themselves. We've all chosen to work with children and we all want to do right by them, but we don't always know how to handle them.

At first, I thought children were small adults. I treated them that way and watched other adults treating them that way. But I also saw that wasn't working for many parents and children. Parents yelled, children cried, and the parents would look at me and say, "I told Sally I had to go to work, so why is she crying?" Then the child would be so upset she might hit another student, and I might get angry and try to correct her behavior by putting her in time-out. But none of those usual things worked.

Everything changed when I began to use The Power, which, at its heart, is a method of speaking and listening to children, and paying attention to their feelings instead of my own.

It begins by my reading the expressions on children's faces, especially their eyes, and paying attention to their body postures. This practice has brought me to a place where I am so in tune with a

> **Children always respond to love.**

child that all I have to do is look at them and I can tell  what's wrong and what they are thinking.

That's how I discovered The Power. I now understand that children are not out to wreck my day, nor do they intend to hurt my feelings. That realization has allowed me to see another side of children which, in turn, has allowed me to calm down and realize I am the adult, and it is my job to help children along in this world. I find the less I fight with myself (meaning, getting upset), the easier this gets.

I find the more I pay attention to a child's feelings rather than getting upset, the more respect I get from each child. Children see I am concerned because I keep reassuring them by repeating my words and behavior, so they can get a clean understanding of who I am and what will be expected of them. I find most of the power I get is because I don't allow a child to fear me; I don't allow anyone to hurt a child; I am honest, respectful and fair; I teach each child how to defend themselves through their own words; and most of all because I care. Children are masters of their worlds and you cannot fool a child for very long, so my leading by example in a healthy way has allowed me to obtain The Power.

The last thing that really helped me to understand children was coming to the realization that every interaction that takes place in my classroom gym has a purpose. There is a reason I act and speak this way: it works best for the child; and that's the secret to the Power. It is doing what works best for the child.

Being in tune with your child and remembering these things will allow you to keep this power. This power only comes to people who pay attention to children and who are willing to teach them with a kind heart. It is impossible to obtain if you are mean, yell, or spank a child, so if you do any of those things, don't even try—you are wasting your time.

## Learning What The Power Will Give You

Everything starts with me feeling comfortable in any situation. When a child does something wrong, I feel I have the skills, the techniques, and the communication abilities to calm them down and allow them to hear me. I let them know that what they did isn't necessarily a "big deal," but I need them to change their behavior. I believe this power also allows me to utilize my word patterns to de-escalate any situation. So when a child is upset or when I'm upset, my using word patterns and correct tones allows the child to understand me and calm down. Then I can get them to pay attention to what they're doing or did. At that point, I can tell them that they need to change their behavior or I will have to control the situation (meaning get involved).

Most children do not want you to take that control because they don't have much in the first place. Many parents are already controlling and demanding and don't give children a chance to have their own voice to tell what they are feeling. When they do tell, they are in fear of you blowing up, going crazy or you hitting or spanking them. In these situations, every single time a child is going to tell you they don't want you to be upset or they don't want you to be angry, regardless of what they did; in fact, most of the time the child isn't even thinking about what they did. The only thing they care about (and I will say this over and over) is that you are scaring

> **The main reason for these word patterns are so your children will start saying these exact words when they feel the need to explain themselves to you or others. This system is based on your children learning how to use these words for themselves.**

them and they want you to calm down. When I have a child who is scared, I calm them down by using words like these: "You don't have to be scared of me," "I didn't mean for my loud voice to scare you," "Use your words to tell me what is wrong," or I will give them a hug while saying these words to try to calm them. Children always respond to love.

After I say these words or go through these situations, my intention is always to correct the problem. Now that the child is calm, I can explain to him why he scared me. These words are meant to allow him to stay focused in the moment. Then, again, I use my word patterns to give him support to tell me what is going on in his mind. He tells me why he has acted in this way; and then in a calm manner, I explain why I want him to stop or correct his behavior.

Eventually, the children will start to understand and trust that what I say protects them. Both the children and I know I'm the one in control of the situation, and the children know I will take care of them. My use of the same words over and over calms them down, reassures them, and gives them hope and confidence. The main reason for these word patterns are so your children will start saying these exact words when they feel the need to explain themselves to you or others. This system is based on your children learning how to use these words for themselves.



When a child acts in a certain way my word patterns lead me to a specific sentence that I say every time. I say the same sentence so the child, over the course of time, realizes what is getting ready to happen. Then children can predict the future. They can predict what I'm going to say and how I'm going to say it just as they do when you hit or spank them. Isn't it weird that they still act in the ways we don't want them to? It is not weird to me; I get why they still do it.

The bottom line is by showing consistency in my language, the children stop testing me. This whole process starts by me being calm, me looking at the bigger picture and me understanding what is really going on in the child's mind. I think that is what helped me the most. I know exactly what the child is feeling or thinking at that moment and I don't want them to continue to feel or think that way. Most parents think their children understand them or their concepts and they do not. (I call this Parent Deception. See Chapter 6.) So I let down my guard, I stop everything I'm doing to let them see maybe I am vulnerable and that I am not going to raise my voice to them. What I am trying to do is teach them. A big learning point for me was when I noticed that children watch me trying to teach them; I'm not scolding them. That is the last key to the power, teaching rather than scolding (more on that in the next chapter). This way of thinking creates The Power and The Power is crucial to everything I do. The best part about this system is that it is easy and fun because now you know what's going on in your child's mind. You engage with your child through the words you use and that will help you to stop guessing!

---



Because I praise children a lot, they gain confidence and self-esteem. The more praise I give to a child, the more respect or, even better, attention I get back. The more understanding I am of children's experiments and tests, and the less time spend punishing, the faster the children rebound. I find parents are so overwhelmed that sometimes they can be overbearing. My attitude is to teach rather than scold. Telling children "I love you" is not enough; you have to show them by being involved in their lives through love and understanding their needs.

# Teaching Rather Than Scolding

The definition of teaching is to impart knowledge or skill to somebody by instruction or example.

The definition of scolding is to rebuke somebody angrily.

To speak harshly is to use words to complain, or find fault with somebody.

Understanding these words helps me to remember what I am really trying to accomplish with children: my goal is to nurture a child's mind, feelings, and heart. With all my years of experiences in this arena I realize how much children remember about how you treat them and it does affect their personality and self-esteem.

In this chapter, you will learn that teaching is easier than scolding. One of the many things I have discovered while working with children is that because I pay attention to their feelings rather than my own, I see their needs much more clearly. I also find the simpler I am in everything I do, the better it works for the child. This process is how children learn how to have respect for someone else. I find when you talk to a child in a teaching manner rather than a scolding manner you will always get a better result. Now I am not saying that scolding or disciplining are bad things because that's how we all learn boundaries. What I am saying is "look

> All of the word patterns and all of the support I try to give children are through teaching, and when you're teaching a child it is hard to feel guilty.

outside the box." Take a better look at yourself and see if you are being fair. The difference between teaching and scolding to me is that children need direction and inspiration rather than being yelled at or being told what to do without explanation.

I teach through explanation. When I explain to a child what I am doing and why, they learn about life and the way I think. I know each child and I pay attention to each personality. When I sit down and talk with a child I can tell how much the child does not understand about my feelings as well as how much they do understand about their own feelings. I have found children do understand a lot when it comes to them, but they cannot relate it back to you or your feelings.



This is where I believe parents get fooled by their children. When a child cannot relate to the feelings of his parents, they get their feelings hurt. They think their child is being bad when in fact they are misunderstanding the bigger picture. Children don't have the capability to understand that other people have feelings. I've watched teachers over the course of many years and I feel parents want their child to be fearful or submissive, because that is how they think parenting is supposed to be done, or that is how a child learns because it was how they were taught. I have discovered this way of thinking does not work for children because the problem never gets solved.

One reason I teach rather than scold is this: I never feel guilty. But when a parent scolds her child, as time goes by, she feels guilty. And I believe this can all go away if the parent chooses to teach their child rather than scold them. All of the word patterns and all of the support I try to give children are through teaching, and when you're teaching a child it is hard to feel guilty. I have also learned that teaching empowers me even more, gives me more clarity, and allows me to see that children really don't understand that you have feelings, too. On the other hand, children will protect their feelings fiercely because that is all they have. It's their only way of expression—that's why they use them so much. In our fast-paced life, they do their best but their best cannot be good enough because they don't have enough life experiences to show them what coping, empathy, and compassion for others are.

When parents can teach rather than scold or discipline, they—yes, you the parent—feel more secure which helps parents understand their child better which will allow them to calm down; that calmness reassures them that they're capable and willing to rectify any situation when things do get out of control. I believe what is necessary are these word patterns and approaching them in this specific way. I've watched teachers over the course of many years use this approach and seen how it worked for them. When I applied it to my program, I thought it was fantastic even though all of this has been trial and error.

Just remember, when you communicate through explanation, you will get a positive result.

*I cannot explain myself as well as I would like, especially when I am scared. This is why I am not always very accurate.*

Please remember when a child is scared and you are aggressive—you scream, threaten, or spank your child—they are not capable of answering questions under stress. Also, children are trying to learn what your words really mean. Even if a child is familiar with a word, they still are not capable of understanding it fully. They only understand the parts that pertain to them in their world. So if you want your child to answer you, they can't be scared. If they are scared, you should understand they are mimicking words they think you want to hear.

## Knowing When Your Child Feels Scared
### (And the Best Way to Respond)

The definition of the word "scared" is to be frightened, feeling full of worry or fear. If any of these things happen, your child is scared:

1. A child's eyes get big when you talk to them or they show a mad face.
2. A child says, "I don't know" and/or shrugs their shoulders.
3. A child gives you a blank stare when you ask a question.
4. A child blames someone else. (Children don't handle responsibility well.)
5. A child lies.
6. A child cries.

You may frighten your child when you do the following:

1. You aggressively touch a child or force them to do something.
2. Your tone is loud when you talk to them.
3. You have a mad face when you talk to them. (Children read facial expressions from birth.)
4. You ask them if they did something wrong or if you accuse them of doing it.

Remember, when you yell, threaten, or spank your child, they get mad. I also believe children never understand yelling, threatening, or aggressive behavior.

**Here are some important tips to remember before disciplining your child:**

1.  Children under the age of seven do not understand the concept of time, so don't punish too long.

2.  Children get mad at you—not at what they did—so you have to address their pain or anger first.

3.  Children will only learn by loss of items they value and not through your anger or frustration. If you get angry, then they are learning through being afraid, which creates their anger, frustration, and feeling sorry for themselves. So you are looking at all the outside behavior and not paying attention to the real problem. They don't understand the difference between anger and fear yet.

4.  Children need you to keep repeating the same behavior before they can trust it. If you are wishy-washy, their behavior becomes whiny.

5.  Children do not understand a lot of the words you use. What you think is understanding is them simply mimicking your behavior and relating your actions to an abstract "meaning." They don't understand the big picture. They do not understand your intentions because they are focused only on their feelings.

6.  Keep in mind that if you physically or mentally hurt your child, it's likely because you have no idea what else to do and it's going to backfire soon!

Why do children keep repeating the action you want them to stop? It is because they generally don't understand your intentions.

## Loud Tones and Facial Expressions

Because my gymnastics program is based on an obstacle course structure, and gymnastics is a very dangerous sport, I have to pay careful attention to every move a child makes even when they are some distance from me. It's easy to scare a child or hurt their feelings because I have to shout to get their attention.

I am able to use words and loud tones in my class without scaring children because I have gone the next step: through my explanation to the children, they realize I am not raising my voice at them but protecting them and that is why they accept it. The calmness of the word patterns I use balances the loudness of my voice: "I'm sorry to talk so loud to you, but you scared me," or "I just needed to get your attention before you hurt yourself. I'm sorry my voice scared you." That brief apology is the golden key because it allows me to put the action back on the child. The child may cry or get mad, but when I apologize the child is more apt to listen to me. Then I can explain what the child did to upset or scare me. I will tell children all the time—in a calm manner—"Just because I use a loud tone does not mean I don't like you" or that they are going to get in trouble. And they believe me.

> When I have a child who is scared, I calm them down by using words like these: "You don't have to be scared of me," "I didn't mean to scare you," "Use your words to tell me what is wrong." Or I will give them a hug while saying these words to try to calm them.

If you still don't believe me, you should test what I am saying to see for yourself. The next time you raise your voice to your child, apologize for your actions (raising your voice) then explain what scared you and why. Then you need to add the only reason why you are getting involved is because you love and have to protect them.

Then use your child's currency (more on that later) and explain to them if they continue the behavior, they will lose things they value. After you have done all these things with a teaching attitude, I promise you will be pleasantly surprised.

Your facial expressions affect your child more than you know. When you get upset or when your child hurts your feelings, your facial expression tells them exactly what's getting ready to happen. From birth, your child has had to read facial expressions to understand you and others. They look at faces before they hear words. So when you get frustrated, the look on your face has a lot to do with scaring your child. If I am calm, my face is going to show it and the child will pick up on it. Then I can communicate through explanation and show the child I care.

I was curious about the connection between facial expressions and words, so I compiled a test. I tested older children to whom I could immediately tell what I was doing and why so they could understand and not be mad or scared. You'll see why that was important.

Below are sentences I would say with a very mean look on my face. Notice that these are positive reinforcements, but some children got scared immediately because they thought they were in trouble and only relaxed when I told them to listen to the words. All the children I tested were eight years of age or older. This is where I discovered children read facial expression and listen for tones more than they listen to your actual words. It is interesting to notice that they pick up on the words they can understand and the rest is your facial expressions and tones. This leads me to believe that children under the age of five don't understand a lot of the actual words I use but rather depend on facial expressions and/or vocal tones. More important, this can make a parent think children understand what the parent is saying.

I would say sentences with a mean look on my face to see if the children were:



48

1. Listening to my words or
2. Reading the expressions on my face or
3. Listening to the tone in which I say them.

When you do this, you must have complete eye contact and you must use a loud tone!

Here is my list of sentences. Use these or come up with your own. Choose positive words and say them with a mean or angry face:

- You did a great job!
- I'm going to tell your mom or dad. I am. I'm going to tell her you were listening to my words!
- I am so proud of you!
- Is there anything I can do for you?

This a great test for you to see for yourself how much your children read facial expression and listen for tones rather than listen or understand your words.


## What Children Understand
### (ages two to five)


At this age, children are very curious, like to experiment, are very mobile and can speak in simple sentences. These children learn most by mimicking what they see and learn how to repeat what adults say and do.

Children are also introduced to school. Learning to share and playing with others is a huge milestone in a child's life. At this age, they have no reasoning abilities or the ability to understand anyone's feelings except their own.

Your duty as parents is to understand children. No matter how smart you think they are or how well they can talk, children cannot understand reasoning. Let me repeat: they are mimicking. Most adults get confused because their children can talk so well and hold themselves so much better than they did when they were young. For example: when a child says "I hate you," it's not *you* they hate; it's the power over them they hate. Children only understand hate as something they don't like or something that makes them sad. Children really don't understand the word "hate" means anything about you or your feelings. In fact, they have no concept of others' feelings. At this age, it's all about them. Their happiness, their sadness, their concerns: *mine, mine* or *me, me.* Children do not understand simple adult words. If it's not about them, they don't get it.

What this means is adults need to be consistent in the words they use and make sentences simple. Discipline should only consist of words and using children's currency. Children don't actually start to understand adult concepts until around the ages of eight to nine.

(At around four or five, children refer to hurting your feelings or making you mad, but they still do not understand the concept. This is mimic behavior, so don't be fooled!)

If you agree with this, you will probably agree that "children have no guilt." They don't know what guilt is and could not care less. When children give you a blank stare, it's not because they think they did anything wrong or bad; it's because you are scaring them and they don't know what to do or say. Most of the time they cry because they see the situation as similar to other situations where you're upset and they cry, you settle down when you comfort them. (Lenny falls down and hurts his arm, begins to cry, and you are right there to comfort him, which seems to settle you.) The child is not thinking "My bad. You busted me so I am going to cry because I did wrong." This never crosses their minds. Maybe they're thinking they want to distract you, but only because you're scaring them, not because they feel guilty. Just remember, if a child feels safe and unthreatened, they will feel more secure with themself and your relationship. That is what you as a parent are aiming for.

Children of this age understand only themselves and that is on a basic level: security. So parents must guard against thinking that their children understand adult words and concepts because they can be fooled by children's good efforts at mimicking.


## What Children Understand
### (ages six to nine)


Adults like to use the concept of time to control children in this age group especially. But after twenty-five years of teaching and working closely with other teachers, I can tell you that children don't understand time the way adults do. I have done two informal studies discussing time with children, and after each study, I have concluded that even children on the upper end of this scale (seven years old) have no clue what time is and could not care less. So when parents use time-out as punishment, it usually means you don't know what else to do. It seems to make the parent feel better or gives them relief, but it just makes children mad. As I said earlier, making the child angry doesn't necessarily work since then the child isn't listening to your explanation and so he isn't learning.

Now, there's nothing wrong with punishment. I understand that time-out is used to set boundaries, but there are other ways to express our intentions using concepts our children can understand.

I believe I have found another way. In my classroom, when a child is misbehaving, I stop everything I am doing and explain to the child why I am upset, or explain I have to protect them because they are doing something wrong. In both situations, I will give them choices: if they have to sit out it is very brief, a couple of minutes at the most. A child isn't going to learn more by sitting out longer. By giving the child another chance—sooner rather than later—they will rebound faster, don't feel down about themselves, and haven't had time to get angry at me or the program. The more choices and the less punishment I give, the better result I get in the long run. To me that is more important than saving my feelings (hard to believe but it's true). As long as the child is not physically hurting himself or anyone else, the softer I am with punishment. *As long as I am consistent*, the more the child respects me and believes what I say. Children respond better because it doesn't make them angry, which allows them to hear my words and know I will protect them and love them. It's not that I'm being easy; I'm being fair.

Children remember how you treat them. Punishing too much can break children's trust and recognizing it is very hard. I find if I give them a serious apology, letting them know I understand I hurt their feelings but it was for a reason—I had to protect them or their actions or body scared me—that shows the child I can be trusted. It is as if they know I was protecting them in a kind way even though they did something wrong. It also lets them know their mistakes are not a big deal. Once your child starts trusting your system, you will see a lot of things change as they grow.

(I do understand there are some children who are either chemically imbalanced or have got to the stage where you have lost control. In those special cases, this concept may not apply until the family gets this under control. Those situations will need to be handled differently.)

## Recognition of Time

This is my "Recognition of Time" test. Ask your six- to seven-year-old child these questions and you will probably discover how little he or she understands the concept of time.

1. Point to a clock and ask, "What time is it?"
2. "How many hours are in a day?"
3. "How many minutes are in an hour?"
4. "Is a.m. in the morning or the night? Is p.m. in the morning or in the night?"
5. "When does the afternoon begin?"
6. "When the sun comes up, is it a.m. or p.m.?"

Please feel free to make up your own questions.

The fun part about this is hearing them guess, realizing through their answers how little they know. But you have to ask and hear answers with no expression on your face. If they answer, move on to the next question. Remember, no expression to reveal that they are right or wrong. These questions are so you can hear your child's answers and their understanding of this word "Time."

So when you say things like…

1. I will be there in a few minutes;
2. I will be home in 45 minutes;
3. I told you to wait a minute;
4. Hold on for a second;

they do not understand your meaning. Don't forget that even references to time are not on their radar. When you say these phrases with an aggressive tone, I believe your child thinks you're being mean.

---

## Apologies, Timing and "I'm Sorry"

Why do I apologize or hug a child after I know I have scared them? I do this because this is what makes everything work.

It is important for you to know I think parents are so overwhelmed in today's world they have lost the concept of what raising a child is all about. Through this apology and hug I have re-discovered how beautiful it is when a child makes a mistake or does something wrong because it gives me the chance to teach, to influence through love and understanding rather than being frustrated and angry. The pure affection of a child appreciating that I didn't raise my voice or threaten but rather taught and inspired through my words and actions was amazing. This simple apology or hug at the right time is priceless and when done right you will know it because your child will start to talk to you instead of cowering down, getting mad, lying to you, giving you a blank stare or mumbling "I don't know."

For me the reason for the apology or hug is to show the child I didn't mean to scare them. Remember, when a child is scared, they are learning through fear. For example, say you have asked your child to pick up their toys, and they don't do it; that makes you upset so you start yelling at or threatening them. The next time you ask your child to pick up their toys they will do it only because

> **A hug or apology is the backbone of almost every-thing I do in my classroom.**

they don't want to get yelled at or spanked, and his is the part I want to help you stop.

In my mind, when you ask your child to pick up their toys they should do it because they understand the reasons: they made the mess as well as they want to live in a clean environment. And they should understand that there are adult reasons why you want them to pick up after themselves. See how there is a difference to the way your child can learn? I think it is time to stop teaching our children through fear and to start teaching them through engagement and using the right words in order to show you care.

## Calming Down, Not Giving In



Just because you give your child a hug or apologize for scaring them doesn't mean you are forgiving them or are overlooking what they did or didn't do. It means you are being kind and sensitive to their needs as a child. You aren't giving in because you feel guilty for punishing them. It doesn't work like that. This is only meant to calm down your child so they can hear and understand why you are taking a certain action, that you are paying attention to their needs, and telling them what is required and why. This is the reason for the hug or apology, but it can also be to comfort a sad and confused child.

Just remember that after I punish a child, I will show them I am sad for them just because I want them to see and know I love them.

For example: I will say something like "I'm sorry you have to sit out. I remember when I had to sit out I didn't like it either."

Plus, it helps them to see that I am not being mean; I'm just being fair and protective. I don't punish very long but rather give the child another chance as long as he understands why I asked him to sit out in the first place. They have to tell me with their own words or by repeating me if they don't know how to use their words yet before I will let them return. Remember, I don't like repeating myself and this helps to stop it. There is nothing wrong with your child seeing you are sad for them. I find this to be a good thing sometimes because it allows the child to show me remorse rather than just being upset at me for punishing them. See how this hug or apology can actually help you understand what your child is going through? This helps keep you from getting upset and becoming aggressive. This hug or apology is the backbone of almost everything I do in my classroom.

*Talking down to me makes me very emotional but most of all it makes me not like you.*

When you talk down to your child you are really hurting your child's feelings, making them feel like their efforts aren't good enough and that will lower their confidence or self-esteem. It also causes them to feel sorry for themselves and they become less likely to want your help or input. I can say from experience, nothing good ever comes of speaking down to a child. When this happens everything you do with this child becomes very emotional. Everything that happens now is done through fear and guessing.

## Timing and Approach

I believe part of the secret of my success is the timing around which I choose to engage with a child when they do something wrong and the approach I take. When I am upset at something a child does, I do not ask them questions about their behavior because I know I will not get an answer. I know this because when I am mad and I ask a scared child why they did something the answers I always get are a blank stare, a shrug, a quick "I don't know" or my favorite, "He or she did it!". To me, none of those are answers. (The answer I'm looking for is "Because I was not paying attention," or "I did it because I didn't think I was going to get caught.")

The first thing I do is correct the problem by telling the child they have to stop. Then I place the child's act back on them by asking if I can do that act to them and then the answer is usually no, as I've described in other areas in this book. By having this discussion, the child understands you are not mad at them; you are just being a parent. After this discussion I tell the child I cannot reward bad behavior and then I apply child's currency (Chapter 6).

When your child gets upset is the time to show them compassion, and it is okay for you to show them you are sad that they have to sit out or lose something they like. I will often tell them I feel sad for them or give them a hug and then immediately say, "If you don't like sitting out or losing something, then stop acting or doing that." Sometimes I follow it up with a hug as well as reminding them the only reason I got involved was because of their behavior. (Their behavior scared me because I am responsible for them.) Sometimes I will ask them again, "Are you sure I can't do that to you?" And again, when they say no, I tell them "That is why I can't let you do it to me or someone else." See how my explanation always helps them to understand it is not me being mean, it is their behavior, and I have to protect them because I would not let someone bother or hurt them. I find when I talk to a child in this way, they understand better. I'm showing

> **When you are inconsistent, I get confused and lose faith in you.**
>
> Consistency is what makes a parent trustworthy. Showing a child that your words, behavior, and attitude are consistent will help them in every part of their lives, but when you are inconsistent, your child has no other choice but to test. They test boundaries, punishment, or fairness looking for and hoping for consistency. Given the choice, most children would choose consistency so they can learn how to predict what you might do or say.

them I care rather than screaming "I told you to stop," or "I told you not to do that." I'm not expecting them to understand at face value (meaning, from my point of view).

*Expecting a child to understand the overall picture through a quick command is how you, the parent, keep making your mistakes.* Children need more input and more consistency in your behavior and communication skills before they can change, and throwing out commands is only making you feel like you are in control when, in fact, you are not. You are really only making it worse because your child is constantly scared of you and is just responding because she is scared.

See how the timing of my approach to the child is different from yours. The time I spend being upset at a child's act is very short. Place the child's act on them, and then use this time to show them why you take this stand that you are here to help and protect them. I have learned that there is a time during a heated moment that a child will listen to you but only if you handle it like I have suggested, and only after the child has calmed down, and their fear has passed.

So, again, between the times when you scared your child (told them to stop) and the time when you apologized for possibly scaring them, is the *only* time you can actually get them to understand what you want instead of what they think they wanted or should have. So timing is crucial. I have just a very small window of opportunity in the beginning of a heated moment to handle it with my words and patience. I know I must get the child to understand I am the adult and there are rules they must follow and there will be consequences for their actions and choices. So the timing of when a child can understand something they have done without getting defensive is in your approach to not scaring them and the timing of your apology if you did.

## I'm Sorry!

Children do not understand what the words "I'm sorry" really mean. They are simply mimicking you because you are the one telling them they have to apologize.

I have watched many boys either hit another child or step on or physically come in contact with another child, and then either say nothing, or turn quickly and say, "I am sorry," turn away and continue what they were doing. The other child's face told me that it was not okay even though the aggressor had said he was "sorry." I have heard many times a child say, "I said I was sorry!" Those words show that the child does not understand what "sorry" means. If he was "sorry" he would not keep doing it and saying "sorry." Understanding other people's feelings is impossible for children under the age of five.

Children believe if they say they're sorry, everything is okay. But if you ask the other person, "sorry don't cut it" (even though sometimes accidents can't be helped). What the other person really wants is for the aggressor to be punished or not allowed to play if the behavior continues. Children need to learn the reason why we say we're sorry. And that reason is because we do not want it done to us. I will give you an example. If a child hurts another in my class, everything stops and the child who was hurt is allowed to say it is "not okay." Then I ask the aggressor if the victim can do that to him. When the aggressor answers it is always "no." Then I ask "Why not? You did it to them." The aggressor always says, "Because that would hurt me." Then I say, "If you don't want them to hurt you, you can't hurt them." Usually when I ask the child who was hurt if the words "I'm sorry" made them feel better, they say "no."

Explaining to children why we pay attention or why we don't hurt others is very important—I get that—but my problem lies in the way many parents do that. I believe if you use your words in a way your child can understand it will go a long way in building their understanding of compassion. Just saying, "You need to say you're sorry" isn't good enough. I would rather the child say something like

"I wasn't paying attention," or "Are you all right?" or "Is there anything I can do for you?" As well as not wanting it done to us, engaging in the other person's feelings is how we need to teach our children why we don't do certain things.

Many times I see parents not taking the time to explain "why". In return children just don't get what you mean and in turn you feel like your child keeps testing you but if you follow the Power method, you address each issue *every time the same way*. Confronting your child's behavior is crucial to their understanding and if done correctly you will see your child blossom because they know what is expected and will not test so much. Trust me this will take a while but is worth it. I have discovered children pick up on confrontations. All my children know if they do something right or wrong there will be a confrontation and they like it. It makes them feel safe because they know I will praise them and protect them with their words and mine.

# Steer Your Child Toward Confidence

## How I Handle Situations in My
## Classroom Can Help You

I want to tell you how I handle situations in my classroom because these are things that may come up between your child and you. It's important for you to know that with a little bit of patience and understanding, all children are capable of doing something they may initially have thought they could not do.

The key is this: when it comes to my classroom, I don't deal with the children based upon my values of what I think they should be able to do; instead, I allow them to move forward at their own pace. That's what I urge you to do. I believe that allowing a child to learn at their own pace gives them personal confidence and self-esteem through their own actions and accomplishments. As a parent you cannot *give* these important things to them. It is something they have to achieve themselves, but you can *help* them through guidance and support.

It is equally important for you to understand what happens if you handle these situations incorrectly and the lasting impression it has

> **Children may act out for a variety of reasons, but the one I never find on the list is they are doing it on purpose because they want to be bad or cause you to get upset.**

on a child. In answering the following questions, I'll  show you how to help your child gain confidence, grasp correct behavior, understand consequences, and grow in understanding.

- What do I do when a child is afraid to do a skill?
- What do I do when a child gets up and runs around?
- What do I tell a child about safety or how to be safe?
- What do I do when a child does not listen to my words?

## Pay Attention to His Fear

When you make your child do something they are afraid to do, you are scaring your child and teaching them to learn through fear. This is based on my experiences and is not a guess.

When a child is afraid to do a skill and I pay attention to the child's fear, that goes a long way toward gaining their trust. Conquering something we fear is hard even for adults. If you feared heights, for example, you wouldn't want someone pushing you around if you were in a high place. So imagine what it's like when an adult pushes a frightened child around.

I learned the hard way. I remember playing with one little boy in my gymnastics class, and he wanted to do a somersault roll for the first time but was afraid. I could tell he wanted to try so I gently grabbed him by the ankles as he tucked his head under and I carefully rolled him over. As soon as I did it, I could tell something was wrong. He didn't get hurt—I checked—but still I knew something was wrong. The next time he came to that station he immediately started saying he didn't want to do it. I said, "Why?" He said, "I don't like that." It took me about two seconds to understand it wasn't the roll, but the way I made him do it.

After the fact, it didn't matter what I did or said; he wouldn't try it again. It took him another two years before he wanted to try it again. That day I learned if a child is afraid, I have to handle it in a safer way.

I learned to begin by explaining what to expect from a classroom exercise, that it would be safe, and that we would go slowly. I also placed my head down on the mat with the child as they rolled over and gave them a lot of praise for accomplishing a skill they were afraid of. I asked them questions about their experience so they could tell me in their own words how happy they were for giving it a try. That allowed me to remind them they could trust me and gave me the chance to tell them how proud I was. That is music to a child's ears.

When I know a child is afraid to do something, or they tell me they do not want to do a skill, I start talking to them in a kind way and I ask them to stand off to the side so they can watch. I choose a child who does do the skill really well, and after that child does the skill, I ask the fearful child if the other child got hurt. I say, "Look at her face; does she have a happy face or sad face?" I ask the child who just did the skill if they got hurt or if I let them fall. When the child says "No," I turn and explain to the fearful child that I will not let her fall, either. Then I say, "This is the way we learn. Everyone has to be taught." While I am helping, I find children notice other children are not getting hurt, which encourages them to give it a try.

Once we go through this process, I usually tell the child they do not have to do the skill. They can just give me a high five or a hug and then I always follow up by saying, "Thank you for using your words; and if you ever want to give it a try, I won't let you fall." I also say, "See what you get for using your words," or "When you use your words it helps me to understand what you want." I always say these phrases with a big smile on my face and with a kind attitude. The biggest thing for me is to pay attention to the child's fear and to let them know that their fear is important to me. I want them to know I am here strictly to help them have fun; and if they do not want to do the skill, it is no big deal. Now my main objective is to have them overcome this fear and, eventually, to get them to do the skill because once they do that, once this fear process happens and the child overcomes it, *it really helps them overcome most other fears they have down the line.* I can use this situation later on to say something like, "Remember when you were afraid to do the somersault roll over the bar and you were able to do it after we worked on it?" I use this as a catalyst.

I am the one helping them. I tell them this is the time they want to try! This is the time that they want to learn!

If you force a child to overcome their fear, even after they are done with the skill and they know they didn't get hurt, they are still scared because it wasn't on their terms. It wasn't under their will; they were not raising their hand saying, "Yes, I want to try this." When they are forced, they remain afraid. Maybe not as much as before, because they did it, but there is still an amount of fear. Now, on top of the fear, you have to deal with the next time that child doesn't want to do something. He or she knows you are going to force them to do it or you're going to be aggressive when you do it.

I start to think, if that was me and you were forcing me to do a skill, I would become very intimidated by you. I would very forcefully say, "No, I don't want to do that, and I don't even want to try because I know you're going to grab me and throw me over the bar. I just know I will be scared." When a child is afraid, this is your time to shine. This is your time to let them know that you are aware they are afraid and their fear is important to you.

See how learning through fear can scare your child? See how being aggressive doesn't work? See how looking at the situation like I do works to the child's benefit? See how important it is to have an open mind and be open to new approaches?

Guess what? I have never had a child who wanted to do a skill not do it because they were afraid.

## Be Consistent with the Testing Child

Children don't know about rules or boundaries until they learn them and that takes some time. Children who do understand about rules and boundaries and still act out are only testing, looking for some kind of attention or direction, or they are angry and don't know how to express their feelings. This is where you will learn how I combat these testing stages—I give you step-by-step instructions so you can take back control of your child.

Children may act out for a variety of reasons, but the one I never find on the list is they are doing it on purpose because they want to be bad or cause you to get upset. Through my discussions with children I have ruled this out. What I have discovered is this is a great opportunity for me to step in and teach a child the importance of correct behavior. As long as a child doesn't have a chemical imbalance, a child who gets up and runs around tells me I need to have a lot of patience, continue to remind them about the rules, and let them know when I will discipline them for their behavior. I know I can never waver because it will confuse these children. Consistency is the key.

When I have a hyperactive child, I understand that I have to be a little more lenient with them. For example, if we are all sitting down on the mat and a child gets up and just bolts and starts to do stuff, everything stops. No one takes any turns; I direct my attention to that child and let them know now is not the time to be running around, and when I call their name it will be their turn to play.

Now I am going to give you a couple of scenarios. A typical one is where I see a child sitting on the mat getting antsy. I call the child's name so they can have a turn and after the child takes their turn, as long as they come back and sit on the mat, I will not make them wait very long before I call their name again. I let the child go a few times extra because I know they're hyperactive. Every child needs different input and/or different dialogue and when a child is hyperactive, you have to let them continue to get their energy out. The only way to do this is to allow them extra turns. When I'm dealing with a hyperactive child, I praise that child a lot when they sit with their hands in their lap as they wait for their turn, or for any other correct behavior. It is important for them to be praised.



There is still another side to this: when the child gets up and runs around, the other children sitting on the mat showing correct behavior are watching my reaction to that child. They need to know the testing behavior is not acceptable. So I have to handle this gently and correctly with a lot of patience, maybe a lot of hugs, telling the hyperactive child I love him and overemphasizing his good behavior. I know a lot of people in his world do not have a lot of patience with him. When a child puts you in a position of being frustrated or angry and you're aggressive with him, you are only teaching him that that behavior is okay.

Sometimes I'm not patient, loving or rewarding when they are sitting correctly, and if I'm not, I know their behavior will only get worse. Because I know the outcome, I realize how fragile my behavior is toward a hyperactive child. If this is to work, I can't mess up because children remember and it is hard to rebuild their trust. If I am not consistent, I can't expect them to be consistent.

### Teach, Don't Scold

The first thing we have to understand is that a child is going to be a child. They are going to test you and your boundaries to see if you will hold your ground. They are testing for holes in your ability to protect and teach them because they're trying to figure out life. I call it their personalities shining through. I understand how important my coping mechanisms and communication techniques are and in order for me to allow a child to grow properly, I have to make sure I don't miss my chance by getting upset. I look at each test as a time to teach and inspire the child rather than scold. One of the ways I do this is to stay consistent with the words I use and never to waver in my punishment.

When a child is not listening to me, something bad is getting ready to happen. So everything stops and I tell the child, first, they are scaring me; second, that I must correct their behavior or I can get in trouble; and third, I'm getting involved only because they give me no choice. Children understand what fear is. They don't like it when adults scare them so it helps them relate to me when I say they are scaring me. I want the child to know I am responsible for them, and if they do something wrong or hurt someone, I can get in trouble. I also let children know it is because I want to that I am getting involved. Their behavior is causing me to get involved. This will also help teach them their actions will create some kind of response from you—good or bad.

My word patterns are simple; it's easy to direct your mind to the ones that fit the situation. So just get used to using these word patterns. They're not repetitious. It isn't tedious because they work.

Repetitious would be saying, "I need you to listen to me. I need you to listen to me. I need you to listen to me!" and the child doesn't listen to me. No. You have to get deeper into it. You have to say the reasons *why* they need to listen to you and what happens if they don't listen to you—consequence and child's currency. Don't do this in a demanding or demeaning way. Use consideration and concern. Remember, you are teaching, not scolding. Don't forget harsh tones and mean facial expressions can scare a child, who will then not hear your words. So again, when we as adults think that by using a few simple words—for example, "Quit doing that," "I told you to stop," "If you do that again I'm going to spank you," "Wait until we get home," or anything in that realm—we're going to get through to our children, no, those are the wrong words. Children need more specific input, more dialogue from you explaining to them the reasons why.



If the child is acting inappropriately, the only way to change the behavior is to get in-depth on a level that children can understand. Taking a couple of seconds to say the same old thing: "I told you to stop," "Why did you do that?" "What were you thinking?" just isn't working. I am letting you know what worked for me countless times. I get the best outcome: not only does the child stop behaving badly but they understand why *and* they love and appreciate me for being the one to show them or explain it to them. It's not like it's taking any more time out of my day. What it's doing is shortening the time I have to spend dealing with this same behavior over the course of time.

Please don't be the parent who says "I have explained it thousands times," or "I don't have the time," or "My child does understand what I am telling them" because if you are, your child's frustration with you will only get worse. If you think the behavior is bad now, think about how much better it can be if you start using The Power now and work with your child to keep these inappropriate behaviors from becoming a habit. For your sake, I hope you listen to what I am saying and start to fix these problems now before it is too late.

## Build Expectation

Often I find it's useful to tell children what is going to happen before it happens. Earlier I mentioned talking to your children about leaving them at the classroom. They understand better when you have told them beforehand why you are leaving them, what you and they will do while you're apart, and when you'll return. Giving them the chance to ask questions and role-play around this topic helps the child understand what's coming so they don't fear it or don't fear it as much. In my classroom, I use the same routine around the topic of safety. I always tell children what to expect before we start, and why. I find the more information I can give to a child, the more it helps them to understand what is going to happen. This action also helps children to remember. The neat thing about my experience is that after children become familiar with my words, they will start repeating them. What I do and say in particular may help you because my main point to you as a parent is that in any new situation—or one a child hasn't faced in a while— you may find yourself addressing the child's fear. In my classroom, the students learn to say, "Use my words, not my hands," "I can get hurt in here," "Be careful," "Wait for my turn," "Don't hurt the person in front of me." That lets me know the children listened and remembered, and that is music to my ears.

So I've learned that letting children know ahead of time what can happen and what my expectations are about their behavior goes a long way toward giving them something to think about, giving them some direction before we start. I feel the more information I can give a child beforehand and the more they repeat the words I use, the better result I get in the long run. For me, that has always been the goal. I also find it is very important at this stage to let children ask questions. Every time we do this repetitive exercise, at the end I always ask if anybody has questions or if they didn't understand any of the words I used.

This is where I learned children do not understand certain words I thought they did. Let me remind you that I've spoken of this before. Children are not little adults. They don't understand adult concepts even though they sometimes mimic the words. I gained a lot of my knowledge about what children could and couldn't understand. In my class, children do not fear me, so they have a way of speaking their mind. I am calm in my demeanor when we're talking in the beginning of class about safety. I find because children feel safe with me they are willing to share information and by sharing with me they learn it helps them.

This next part lets me know how much the children understand after we are done repeating. While the children are playing I test them to see if they understand what I just said by asking questions like: How many people go on the trampoline at a time? Can you hurt your body in this class? Are you allowed to hurt or kick the person in front of you? Will I let you fall? These questions are meant to keep the child focused and in the moment, because if they become silly or stop paying attention, someone will get hurt. This also helps the child to start communicating so they can become more comfortable with me.

When I started asking questions, I learned how much children really didn't know, understand, or pay attention. I was surprised how many words I used that children didn't understand. I discovered most children never asked what a word meant unless I asked first so that led me to believe children do a lot of acting and following rather than leading or paying close attention. I find children are not willing to ask questions when they don't know because they are scared of upsetting adults. I find most children don't even know how to ask the right questions because they are worried the parent will be demanding and aggressive. It's important to ask your child in a calm, quiet way if they understand the words you used and know what you said.

Build expectation by telling your child as much beforehand as you can so the child is ready for the situation. Let them ask questions, be calm so they feel they can ask you questions, make sure they understand your words, and help them ask questions they might not know how to ask. Reassure them that you can help them through any fear they have. The key is for you not to put an emotional value on the lesson. It's just about the action. For example, when I correct a child's behavior, that's all I'm focusing on and all I want her to focus on: an action that will correct a problem. I want her to concentrate on that action alone. I don't let my emotions get involved until after my explanation, once the behavior is corrected. Once that is done, I'm ready to hug and say, "Thank you for using your words," or "I'm sorry you had to sit out. I can't reward bad behavior." Then I follow it up with

"Thank you for using your words and telling me what you need or did." It's important to drain the lesson of its emotional value and correct the behavior. Then you can add the emotion back in.

---

# A Child's Currency

## Give Them Choices—Lots of Choices

I give children a lot of choices because it allows them to think for themselves. When children are given choices, they get to be in control. They are held accountable for their choices because it was their choice and no one else's. Children learn so much from choices because they are choosing who they are. Individual choices are what define us as individuals now, and eventually, who we will become. Children need to learn that with choice comes consequence and consequence is how we learn the rules of life. We choose to do the right thing because we don't want to go to jail, and we choose to be kind because we don't like it when someone hurts us. I could go on forever. See how giving children choices instead of just telling them what to do is so important, and being a dictator doesn't work?

Children like to be led by example, so when we make bad choices as adults we show our children that bad choices are okay. If you expect your child to be held accountable, then you have to be held accountable first and show them how it is done because if you don't, they will know.

Choices can be as simple as: if you choose to behave I will reward you by doing something you like, or as complicated as: if

> Children's Currency is not money. It is whatever is valuable to your child.

you choose to do well in school I will reward you by letting you go out with your friends. Choices are how we learn if we can trust our children when we are not around and choices are how we learn about our children's behavior. Choices are something children cannot live without, so please allow your child to make a choice and not be dictated to. Allow them to be in control through their choices.

## Let Children Know There Are Consequences for Their Choices (Good and Bad)

If you are engaged with your child, I think it is important for you to explain about choices and consequences to your child outside of discipline, within the confines of your normal day. I find the more you talk about choices, the better chance your child will believe you when you bring up the word "consequences." Children are constantly testing so it will do you good to stand your ground and help them by letting them know they have choices and that with those choices come consequences. Use words like "I will give you a choice," or "If you choose to . . . there will be a consequence." You get the idea. You and your child should talk about choice and consequence all the time.

Here are some examples:

- I let children know they have a choice by asking them what they want. By making a choice, they exercise their ability to learn how to make choices.
- I tell them after they make a choice that was their choice. They chose to make that decision.
- I let them know I will hold them accountable for their choices.
- I will ask them if they are sure that is the choice they want to make, especially if they are doing or getting ready to do something wrong.
- I tell them it was their choice when they do something wrong (or right). Then we talk about that choice.

- Lastly, I either congratulate them on their choice or, if they did something wrong, I will use child's currency by telling them they made a bad choice and I cannot reward bad behavior.

## Children's Currency

Children's currency is not money. It is whatever is valuable to your child.

When you use children's currency, *you must be consistent.* Children start to learn how to predict as long as they can predict with 100% certainty.

Say, for example, when your children do something wrong or break rules, you correct them, right? Well, most of the time you scare them. Once I have noticed I have scared a child, I always address her feelings. I say calmly, "I did not mean to scare you," or "I did not mean for my words to scare you." If I do not say these words, I get a completely different result—the child thinks I am being mean. As soon as this happens, the child is learning through fear and that is the reason for the apology or hug. I apologize and hug her so she can hear what I really want and that is for her to correct her own behavior.

Remember, most confrontations scare children. You have to be calm when teaching children if you want them to remain calm and listen to your words. Once you accomplish this calmness, you will see what I mean. Your child will stop being scared and start to talk to you rather than giving you the blank stare or shrug. Just knowing I'm scaring them and that they get mad when they're scared helps me calm down because I realize being aggressive in any way doesn't work with children. Children are still learning what words mean and it takes time and a great deal of explaining for them to trust what you are saying. I feel that leading by example is what has helped me the mostin the classroom. Children need to look up to their parents rather than fear them.

I hope this information will allow you to feel like you are equipped with knowledge you didn't have before so you can now handle behavior problems correctly.

## Child's Currency
### (ages three to five)

Remember that the definition of child's currency is discovering anything your child likes, likes to do, places they like to go as well as things they do not like to do or places they do not like to go. The most important part about using your child's currency is you can never waver in your punishment, and if you do, then you've wasted your time and, most of all, you've confused your child. You have to learn to be prepared for whatever your child does emotionally, and you cannot waver even if your child continues to scream, cry, or throw a tantrum. You have to be strong and know that what you are doing is right because the opposite of this is being aggressive—and you have now discovered with my help what really goes on in a child's mind when you are aggressive (i.e., they feel scared, angry, frustrated, sorry for themselves, and they begin to learn through fear). I think sometimes when parents are aggressive with children it is as if the parent feels better and that is just wrong.

Now when a child does something wrong or breaks a rule, you have to take something away from them which they value (currency) and then you have to let them know why. I also let them know I am getting involved because their behavior forced me to and not because I want to. (Telling children they scared me helped me a lot.)

Please let them know what they should have done and don't forget to add if they do it again this will be the result *every single time*.

At this age, children are overlyemotional and cry easily because they can't defend themselves or communicate well. Tell them you cannot reward bad behavior. Tell them you are teaching them about behavior and give them examples like "Would it be okay if I did that?" or "Would I get in trouble if I did that?" to help them understand they've made mistakes. (Just remember children at this age do not understand what the word "behavior" means. They have to learn it over the course of time. So keep using it.)

Children at this age will feel sorry for themselves. This means that when you punish them they feel you are being mean and that makes them mad. Examples: They will start to cry or whine. They will blame someone else. They will deny it. They will say, "You hurt my feelings" or "You made me sad." They will say, "I hate you" and sometimes you will hear it and sometimes you won't, but they are thinking it. You can tell by the look on their faces. I know you have seen this look before. Don't forget this is how they defend themselves because they don't have the communication skills to tell you yet.

In order for this to work, you have to commit to taking time at the time the child is showing incorrect behavior, and you can never waver in your punishment. The last thing, but the most important one, is you cannot punish through threatening them.

*When you yell, threaten, or spank (hit) me I get scared, then mad. I stop thinking about what I did and start thinking about what you just did.*

This is the reason children get mad at you for punishing them. If they can't understand the reason you are punishing them, then your choice of punishment isn't working at all. Children need to understand that when they make a mistake or break a rule *that* is the reason you are getting involved. If you continually think your child understands the way you are treating them then just know you are raising a scared child.

I think it is important for you to know this because this is how I will get you to change the way you look at disciplining your children. If you look through my eyes you can see that addressing your child's feelings about scaring them must come first. Then you can explain why you got involved. If this process doesn't take place as part of discipline, I believe your child does not understand you and will become afraid of you.

Threatening is negative parent behavior. You do this because you don't know what else to do. Let the child be a child and when they do something wrong, then punish, but with explanations. Tell them you were protecting them, or that they could get into trouble. Talk about rules, and ask, "Would you like it if it was done to you?"

Here are some examples of child's currency for children ages three to five:

- Take away a favorite toy or, better yet, make them give it away.
- Take away TV or video time. (Saturday mornings)
- Make them sit with nothing to do. Cause them to be bored. You have to make the time for this to work.
- Take away structured play times. (Things like McDonald's®, Chuck E Cheese®, the park, playing with their friends, birthday parties, etc.)
- Take away anything they like to do or any place they like to go.
- Take away treats or candy they normally get.
- Take away story or reading time.
- Take away fun things they do at school, like recess.
- You have to find the things they value and use it as your currency.
- If a child is uncontrollable, I would take everything they own or value away and make them earn it back or make them give it away to friends or charity. They would only be allowed to go to school and come home. This should only be done in certain cases. I just want to let you know how extreme this can get. It is okay if you have to take everything they own away. Trust me when I say this will work if you don't waver.

Keep in mind that from the ages of three to five, children respond to punishment differently from children ages six to ten.

## Child's Currency
### (ages six to ten)

Your child's currency will continue to change as they get older so you have to continue to stay in tune with the things your child does and doesn't like. Below is a list of child's currency so you can get an idea of what I am talking about. The definition for child's currency is discovering anything your child likes, likes to do, places they like to go as well as things they do not like to do. The most important part about using your child's currency is you can never waver in your punishment because if you do, you will be wasting your time. Most of all, you will be confusing your child. You have to learn to be prepared for whatever your child does emotionally, and you cannot waver. At this age, children value things more so using your child's currency becomes more dramatic and you have to be prepared for this.



When I say dramatic, I mean your child is going to feel that you are being extraordinarily mean. Remember, their defense is always to get mad. I find because they are getting older their possessions and time become more important to them. Although at this age children remember more about punishment, they are less likely to repeat bad behavior when you use this currency rather than becoming aggressive. You have to be strong and know that what you are doing is right because the opposite of this is being aggressive. By now you have discovered, with my help, what really goes on in a child's mind when you are aggressive (i.e., they feel scared, angry, frustrated, sorry for themselves, and they begin to learn through fear). Sometimes when parents are aggressive with children, it is as if the parent feels better and that is just wrong. I find at this age children are more apt to respond favorably to child currency rather than aggression. Yelling, screaming. or threatening does not work, and if you try it, you will have a very rebellious teenager on your hands. I remember being rebellious because I felt my parents didn't listen to me, they didn't pay attention to my needs, and were unfair, so it didn't bother me when I didn't listen to them.

Now the last thing I want to emphasize is that *when using child's currency you cannot threaten.* ("Threatening" for me is negative parent behavior. You do this because you don't know what else to do and I find this to be very bad.) If your child makes a mistake or breaks a rule, they will soon learn something they like will be taken away as a consequence of their action. I find most children at this age aim to please. They are still children but are starting to get the hang of certain things (going to school, understanding about work, socializing, beginning to realize people have feelings, becoming more familiar about rules and time), but it's your job to remember communication is not one of them.

Here are some examples of your child's currency for six to ten years of age:

- Take away favorite toys or make them give their toys away.
- Take away TV or video games.
- Take away things in their room they like. (Pictures, photos, drawings, etc.)
- Take away friends' birthday parties.
- Take away the phone.
- Take away sports/hobbies. (Extra-curricular activities)
- Take away the computer.
- Take away friends coming over.
- Take away objects. (Bicycles, outside toys, playtime, recess)
- Make them do extra house chores.
- Make them get up early or go to bed early. (Lots of sitting around)
- Make them do extra schoolwork at home on the weekend. (Math or history questions)
- Make them volunteer their time to a needy organization. (People less fortunate)

- If a child is uncontrollable, I would take away everything they own or value and make them earn it back or make them give it away to friends or charity. They would only be allowed to go to school and come home. This should only be done in certain cases. I just want to let you know how extreme this can get. It is okay if you have to take everything away. Trust me when I say this will work if you don't waver.

Just remember—using your child's currency is a great way for you to calm down and realize you do have control of your child if you choose to and that disciplining can be done in a healthy way for you and your child.

## Some Real-Life Scenarios

These are some examples of scenarios I have seen many times in the past.

1. It is 5:30 p.m.; you get off work and go to your child's school to pick them up. When you get there, you tell the child, "Come on, it's time to go." But the child isn't ready to go or is still having fun, so they ignore you. Then you start to get mad or upset and start to scream out threats; if that doesn't work there is always the aggressive grab or slap on the back of the head or butt followed by a mean tone. Ever done this before?

2. Let's say you have been asking your child to clean their room or pick up their toys and it just is not getting done in a timely manner. So you start to get upset. The next thing that happens is you start to yell at your child and threaten to spank or ground them if they don't do it right now. Ever done this before?

Now I am going to tell you what is going on in your child's mind and what they are thinking when you act this way. I am going to tell you why this happens and what I do instead of being aggressive. I will explain to you why I do this and why it is so important that you stop doing what you've been doing. I will explain what message you are really showing your child and what it can do over the course of time.

Your child isn't worried about the outcome; that's why this happens most of the time. Sometimes they do it because somewhere in your daily life you ignore them and they are just repeating your behavior. In either case, it's because you're not sending the right message to your child. You are not being consistent with your discipline, and you are not communicating with your child in a way they are respecting. Again, in either case you allow these types of actions to happen.

Please remember that children think about themselves first, and as a parent it is your job to break them out of this cycle. Children have a hard time seeing the bigger picture because they still don't understand why you do the things you do even after you have explained it to them. Children do not learn through words until they get much older. Children learn through what they can feel right now. Children can't see or understand your schedule or time frame. They just are not capable yet. So you have to teach them in a different way and that way is as follows.

In my world, I understand that I must stay consistent and talk about why I am asking a child to do something. It is because I don't want things like this to happen. Through my engagement and respect, I expect each child to be held accountable for their actions because I hold myself to that standard. This alone will keep a child from disrespecting me because I do not disrespect them. I find because I act this way it really helps the child to relate to me and what I need from them. I find if I respect them first and hold myself to a higher standard (meaning pay attention, not punish too long, help them gain a voice, see me take the lead, and lead by example) each child gets the comfort to be a child and starts to learn through respect and kindness instead of selfish demands because their voices aren't being heard.

If you want misbehavior to stop, you must take the time to explain what you are asking of them and why. And after that if they choose not to respect you, you must have a solid currency plan and never waver. As long as you hold yourself to the same standard you are holding your child to this will work, but if you waver or are inconsistent then things like this will keep happening.

Lastly, I find children remember how you treat them, especially if you are not being fair. Not being fair will get you in more trouble with your child than you can handle. Being fair is what accountability is all about. Don't forget, children get their feelings hurt easily and when you are not fair your child will begin to mistrust you. Things like this will cause your child to ignore you or want to stress you. Children hold grudges when people aren't fair because they remember. I find that children treat me as I treat them, and I will never accept anything less. So, again I say, this is happening because you are letting it happen.

## Taking the Time at the Right Time

I want to let you know that in my twenty-five years of teaching gymnastics I have observed and interacted with over 10,000 parents (probably more), and one thing I often see is that many people are not capable of raising a child without some kind of foresight, some plan of how they are going to raise that child. Nor have they considered the coping skills or mechanisms they'll need as the child grows up and makes their own choices.

When the child does things a child is going to do, how are you going to react to that? I don't see a lot of people going into child parenting classes; I see the majority of the people having children and hoping for the best!

A parent doesn't see things clearly a lot of the time because the parent does not engage with the child at the right time in the right manner. I think the biggest problem for parents is they don't take or have the time to address the issue correctly at the time that it's happening while at the same time that child is not getting the correct direction from the parent when they need it. I think this makes the parent believe their children understand when they don't or expect them to understand when they can't.

Too often, parents don't take the time to engage their child in the way I explain in this book, but instead, just shout out a command—"I told you to stop!" or "How many times do I have to tell you!" or "Do it now!" And leaving it at that, they expect their child will change. In my world, that simply does not work. I do not have the luxury of allowing that behavior.

If I need a child to stop doing something, I explain to the child that they are scaring me (children relate to fear), the reason why they are scaring me (because I am responsible for them), the reason I need them to stop (because I don't want them to get hurt or get into trouble), and that if they continue I will have to get involved (meaning I will use child's currency). I call these steps a *sequence*.

I take these steps every single time because I want the child to get used to me saying these exact things, following through in these exact ways, and producing the same exact outcome—ultimately, that the child is listening to my words and their behavior is corrected. I also believe that is what a parent is striving for: that their children listen to their words.

Using these word patterns takes the guesswork out of parenting. It allows the parent, through their own words, to see how little the child knows. I know when the child doesn't know or understand something because I engage the child. I ask numerous questions, or I will ask the child how they are feeling at that time. Sometimes, by the look on their face, I can tell how they are feeling at that time, and I tell them they don't have to feel that way; if they use their words and talk to me, I can make it better.

From my point of view, some parents are like dictators. They tell the child how they are going to be rather than explaining to the child why they need them to be that way. My observation is that that dictator style or method doesn't work. I call it a "quick fix." It only fixes it for the moment and nothing long-term gets accomplished. Please try to remember, if your child keeps "misbehaving," in your words, most likely it's because they don't understand you or what you are asking from them.

As soon as you stop believing your child understands everything you do, the sooner you can get on the Power track and stay in control of your child. I know if I can do these things with a child and get the results I have, then you can, too. But it all starts with you acknowledging that what you are doing could be hurting your child and that you must give it up.

## Parent Deception or Disconnecting

This is what I believe happens when a parent thinks their child understands their words, behavior or the way they try to teach them. I believe the parent creates the outcome and meaning. If the parent could look at the overall picture or looked outside the box, as I say, they would see what confusion they cause their child when the parent controls them, forgets to give explanations, or thinks the child already understands. As a parent you become blinded because that's your child, your flesh and blood, your living descendant.

I have noticed with just about every parent that that special bond makes them feel their child is better than other children when, actually, they are not. They are just like every other child, a child. Just because a child came out of you does not make them special. It only makes them special to you, so please remember that. Our jobs as teachers, coaches and educators are what our names say we are and we don't need you telling us how special your child is; let us tell you how special they are.



When parents think their child understands when the child really doesn't, I call it parent deception by his or her own belief system. Parents hurt their children when they

1.  Become blinded to what they are doing or saying to their child or

2.  Are of the mind-set that this is the way it is going to be or

3.  Say, "This is the way I am going to do it because I said so."

This way of thinking just does not work with a child. If you could look outside the box, you would see that over the course of time, this way of speaking or thinking actually hurts your child because they can't see the big picture and the outcome. They just think you are being mean. It's very hard to explain. I just know I have seen it through the years. It is what you are doing right now. When you use my methodology and word patterns, you won't ever think that way again. It will train you to become more observant and kinder, but with a backbone, and your child will thank you for it.

Part of the misunderstanding, I believe, is either the parent is disassociating from the reality of their relationship to their child or disconnecting themselves from the situation altogether. Plus, they are looking at the situation from only their own point of view and that can never be good. As a person who works with children, I understand how the pressures of life can create those blind spots. But because you are a parent, you have to be held to a higher standard. When we disconnect from a situation, the bottom line is we stop thinking as individuals and we just start acting; this is bad because you stop feeling. Again, the way this world works is very fast-paced, and it creates in us the need to act rather quickly. But as this book continues, you will hear me ask you over and over and over to slow down, to calm down. And if you don't, none of this is going to work.

When you disconnect yourself from what your child is doing or involved in, the danger is that they will start to believe you don't care or are not interested in them. Now what this does is make the child stop engaging with you, and they start to lose the ability to connect with others in an honest and meaningful way. This happens because you aren't teaching them how, by connecting yourself. Instead they try to please other people, hoping to get some kind of connection. But the only people a child can truly learn about the authentic self from is you, the parent and sometimes an older sibling. Why I say this is because, when a family member engages with you, it teaches you how to learn to voice your opinion and/or to share your feelings. Sharing your true feelings and having them accepted or heard by your family is how we learn to be honest with ourselves about our feelings. It teaches us to express how we feel about each other. So when you don't engage, I believe your child loses the ability to share their true inner feelings with anyone out of fear of not being accepted.

For me the definition of connecting or connection is to get involved in a person's life by being engaged in their feelings, by showing compassion as well as understanding what they need from you as an individual or parent or sibling. Sometimes just listening is good enough.

Please don't think what I am asking from you is going to be easy, either. Just know with the right help and information, anything is possible. You must have the will to learn and change in order to help your child by engaging with them in a meaningful way through allowing them to express how they truly feel.

What follows is a question-and-answer "game" I have done countless times with my students. During the time I spend with children while they are playing—and therefore distracted, so they *don't think* about their answers—I ask them questions about me: if they liked the way I spoke to them, if they were having fun, or how it made them feel if I hurt their feelings. When I got their answers I could tell they were being honest, and they weren't afraid I was going to punish them for their answers. It seemed to be because they were distracted. This leads me to believe it would be a great time for you to talk to your child while you are in their play time. Below is a list of questions you can ask your child about how you are "doing as a parent." If this is done correctly, I believe they will tell you almost anything you want to know about them or you. Remember, when they tell you, you *must not* get upset at anything they say. This is a time for listening and/or explaining and not a time for you to get your feelings hurt.

These questions should only be asked when your child can be distracted by what they are doing, for example, playing with blocks, coloring and/or play time with you. Your tone and facial expressions should be neutral, as if you are asking them a regular question. You should never show any expression except a smile. Say, "Thank you for using your words," then ask questions about their answers.

1. "Do you like it when Mommy/Daddy uses a loud voice when we talk to you? Yes or no?"

2. "Do you know why I used a loud voice?" (I want you to hear them tell you why and/or to see if they will actually tell you.) Sometimes they do know and will say, "Because I was bad" or will answer in a question, "It was too high?" or "Don't do it again?" You know they don't know or are guessing because they ask a question back to your question. But most of the time they will say, "No."

3. "How does it make you feel when I do … or did…?"

4. Now the next questions can be "Do you know what the word bad means? Yes or No?" or "Do you know what the word punishment means?" or "Do you know what… means?"

5. When possible always ask Yes or No after a question. Then when they answer, you can ask, "Do you know why?"

6. I also use this yes and no questioning when I know the answer to my question will be yes. When I ask them a yes or no question, it's because the last word the child hears is "No." If they really are listening to you, they will say "Yes" and not just repeat the last word they heard you say (No). For example, in my class when we are finished I will

ask each child if they had fun—"Yes" or "No"—and I put a big emphasis on NO. I will even shake my head No while they are looking at me with big smiles on their faces and when they say, "Yes, I had fun," I know they are telling me the truth and not just repeating the last word I said! Sometimes a child says, "No" then waits a second and says, "Yes!" Part of the reason I do this is if a child did not have fun or if something is bothering them the way I emphasize the word No gives them an easy opportunity to tell me a real and honest answer. That opens it up for me to address their feelings. I ask them questions about why they are sad and because I do it in a calm manner, they tell me.

Start learning to ask questions kindly: put a smile on your face while doing this. You're doing this to get a better understanding of your child and to see for yourself how your child thinks. You're also learning how much of the big picture they don't understand. This whole book is based on seeing for yourself, through your own engagement, what your child understands and what he doesn't. That is how I did it, and it will be the only way for you to see and learn the same things.

## Giving Children a Voice

Ever wonder why when you say something harsh or angrily scold a toddler they will say "NO"? Ever wonder why, as your child gets older, when you discipline them they will say things like "I hate you," they will get mad at you, they will think you are being mean or will tell you "That's not fair"? It's because they can't see the big picture. They aren't looking at it from your point of view. They are showing you through their words and actions they are concerned about themselves, and are wondering why you are not giving them what they want. Now on top of that they may also be reacting to your being aggressive with them, or perhaps you are not being clear and/or consistent in your discipline. In other words, you don't know what to do or say when your child does something wrong!

Now I believe this is all happening because you're not allowing your child to have a voice so they can tell you what is going on in their mind and/or how they are feeling. If you knew what your child really thought, you would be surprised. Scaring your child causes them to shut down and not be able to speak. This is why I give children a voice. It's because I want them to learn it is okay to talk to me and one of the best ways to do this is to use their words. I want children to feel comfortable telling me anything. I tell children I want to know because I care about their feelings, and if they don't tell me I won't know. I can't read their minds.

The definition of giving a child a voice is helping a child to defend themselves through the words they use and never to be scared to tell me anything, no matter what. It also allows me to introduce *my* feelings.

Everything I say and do is for a reason, and when a child tests me I have an answer for them. My answers are always based upon correcting the problem. I do this by engaging the child with questions and taking the time to talk to them so I can give them the right answers instead of taking what they did personally. For example, here are some questions I will ask after a child has done something: "Why are you doing that?" "Did you forget the rules?" "Is that safe?" "Why didn't you ask me?" "What happens to me if you get hurt?"

Or, I will say, "I need you to use your words, not your hands, if I hurt your feelings or make you upset."

Engaging with your child by talking and showing them you have to protect them can be done calmly. You have to remember your child is still learning even though you have told them many times not to do something. Or when they are doing things a child does, you have to realize the way you have been handling it is old-school. Remember, this technique I am talking about is new-school. You have to start looking at things from your child's point of view or their behavior is never going to get any better.

When you want to talk about your feelings, there is a way you have to go about it and it's probably not the way you have been doing it. Here is an example of what I would say in order to explain to a child that they were hurting my feelings. First, I would ask them if it is okay if I step on their feet? Then I would say, "I need you to use your words and tell me if that would be okay." When they answer "No," you have to ask them, "Why not? You stepped on my feet." Their answer will always be, "Because I wouldn't like that" or "That would hurt me." Then you have to say, "I didn't like that, either," or "When you step on my feet that hurts my body, too." This is how you introduce the fact that you have feelings.

After this process has been done, you can explain to them about consequences. You can say these words as an example: "Because you are choosing this behavior you are giving me no choice but to punish you" (refer to using Child's Currency, previous chapter). Asking them questions like "Do you know why I am acting this way?" or "Do you understand I will have to punish you?" and letting them answer will help you understand how your child thinks. You may have to help them answer by saying, "No, I don't understand," or "Yes, I did do something wrong. I know I will be punished." If they give you a blank stare, you may have to describe their action so they can use your words to find their words. Remember always to place the action back onto the child as the reason you are getting involved.



I think it is important for all parents to hear their child's own *words* about how they feel concerning what you are doing so you can hear for yourself how they *think*. When your child says, "I hate you," starts to throw a fit, gets really upset at you, and/or thinks you are being mean, I believe it's because your words are confusing and scaring them. Plus, you may think they understand adult concepts when they don't. Also, you may not be listening or believing them when they tell you their answer. So, again, I believe if you can calm down and not get your feelings hurt because of something your child did to you, it will allow you to see through my eyes and start to understand how important it is to give a child a voice.

Another example of how I give children a voice occurs when a child is hurting another child or a sibling or me. For me, the action is always stopping that situation, always creating the situation to be talked about (addressing all parties involved), and always resolving the problem. Now, the point I am trying to make is that the child who got hurt is the one defending her ability to tell the other child these things:

1.  They did not like that

2.  That was not acceptable

3.  That hurt their body

4.  The other child should use their words not their hands

5.  If they do that again they are going to get in trouble. (Meaning there is going to be a consequence for the other child.)

Allowing the child who got hurt the ability to defend herself is the reason I start this whole process. I let them see me take control and then I allow the child to take control by literally giving that child the words to say to the other child. I have them repeat my exact words, words like, "I didn't like that," "You hurt my body," or "Can I do that to you?" Sometimes I will allow the child who got hurt to tell the other child they have to sit out and watch for a couple of minutes.

Giving your child the proper words to use helps them to express how they feel and most of all, to tell the other child themselves with our words (i.e., with a lot of help from me with my words) how they felt.) This is the true power behind this whole process—giving your child the words, which allows them to express their thoughts. It sounds like what I'm saying is tell your child what to say, and that you're not really letting your child express herself. But what I've learned is that, for a while, children need help to put words to their thoughts.

I have also discovered that if you let children defend themselves, it teaches them why they should not do an action in the first place.

I have noticed in my many years of working with children that children do pick up on stuff like this quickly. It's as if their own words are teaching them through their own life experiences. We adults call this full circle. Giving your child a voice truly is a beautiful thing to see, as I can proudly say. But parents, please never forget, just because your child relates to their feelings like a pro doesn't mean they relate to your feelings very well at all. So please don't let your child's actions bother you; you have to remember that if they truly understood, they would give you that respect or at least try to.

## Paying Attention

Paying attention is what I do. Because I have paid attention to everything a child does, I am rewarded with the ability to see them differently, to see a side of children I did not expect. The purity of their hearts—due to having trust from birth—is for me the essence of life. To damage that with hostility or through anger is to feel its painful effects later in life. That is why we have scars that stem from how we were treated by our parents when we were young. Because we cannot go back and fix it, I want to start at the beginning to change it and it all starts with me. When it comes down to it, I am the one in control and if I get it wrong it has a domino effect. I have seen, through my own experiences with children, how delicate their feelings are and how easy it is to scare a child. So paying attention to a child when they are young is becoming more crucial as I learn more about them.

Take these words of wisdom and know what you are doing with your child today will have an impact on them later in life. So please show a lot of patience now when they need it the most. As a parent, you will realize the more you pay attention to your child's needs and help them with their words the more you understand what your child does and does not understand.

## All Children Want to Be Accepted

Here is another example of how your child is thinking. All children want to be accepted all the time and when you act aggressively toward a child, they feel you don't like them anymore. I think children feel that everyone is against them when someone is being aggressive with them. I believe that is why I started to apologize when I saw I had scared a child. I could see they thought I was being mean and the only way I found around that was to apologize, with an explanation. This is when I discovered I could break a child out of the "blank stare" or being scared of me and it was simply done with an apology for scaring them. Once I apologized, it did not matter what the outcome was for the child; they always seemed to accept it better.

Now don't get me wrong: they were still upset, but it was in a different way. They were upset with themselves. This is where I learned it is better to punish for a shorter amount of time. This is where I learned if I punish too long, I get a negative response from the child after their punishment. This is where I learned children respond better when given a second chance sooner rather than later. This is where I learned children remember how you treat them. This is where I learned that when it comes to a child's feelings they understand themselves first. This is where I learned children do not understand that other people have feelings.

The point I am making is, I have obtained this information because I was curious and asked questions in a safe environment. I engaged with children under the right circumstances, and they told me anything I wanted to know about how they were feeling. It was because I accepted them for themselves and paid attention to their needs rather than my own feelings. I didn't take it personally when a child did something to me. What I did was learn how to talk to a child so they could understand what is going on and why, what will be expected of them and why. They began to understand that if they broke any of the rules or hurt someone, there would be a consequence. I would also tell them "Just because this is happening doesn't mean I don't like you," or that it didn't mean they were not my friend. It meant only that they didn't listen to my words or didn't follow directions. That was all. Again, I am accepting them for themselves. I'm not placing my values on them and what they did. I am not telling them how to be. Then, once I set these boundaries, I never wavered. Once I learned how to accept a child, I started to learn that children relate to you better if you are fair and respectful even when you have to punish them.

Just because your child does something you don't like doesn't mean you have to take it personally. We need to learn to accept our children for who they are. If you can learn to accept your toddler or preschooler, you can learn how to see things from their perspective. If you can learn to accept your teenager, you can really find out who they are instead of them always telling you to keep out or leave them alone. As long as you are fair and respectful, the outcome, I find, is always better.

In my experiences of watching children, I've learned one thing about all children: they watch out for themselves always. Say, for example, there is a group of children playing with one another and one child is being either aggressive or disruptive. There often comes a point when the other children will not accept their behavior and will tell the child to go away. I have noticed that the disruptive child often says to the group, "You aren't my friend" with a mean face and they walk away. When this happens, it proves to me that the shunned child isn't thinking they did anything wrong to the group; they are upset at the group's actions. They immediately protect their feelings first. This is one of the reasons why I understand how

> **Please listen to me. I have a lot to say. I need you to be patient with me because I am still learning.**
>
> Children really like it when you listen to them because it makes them feel important or that what they have to say is interesting to you. Children are always looking for attention and this is a safe way to show it to them and learn about them. Learning how to listen to a child is how I learned so much about them.

important it is to accept all children and their behavior. If you don't, one of their attitudes could be "You are not my friend!"

I hope this information will help you come to a point where you can say, "Oh, that's why," or "Oh, I didn't know that!" and make it easier for you to realize how your child thinks so you can learn the skills or techniques I use to de-escalate any situation. I want to teach you techniques so you can feel comfortable with yourself because what you are learning is healthy for your child. I am confident your child will show you how well this works by listening to your words and, most of all, learning from your direction.

It's hard sometimes to accept your child for who he or she is because you want to shape them into your idea of a "good child." But if you don't make an effort to accept them, this builds anger at the parent (as friend) and ultimately no one is the child's parent.

Remember that in order to give children their voice we have to be calm with the child because a scared child won't speak. Engage them with questions. Talk about feelings: theirs and yours. Remind them about consequences. Help children use their voices by giving them the proper words they need at a particular time. Pay attention to their feelings and accept them for who they are.

---

## Word Patterns

> **How to use word patterns, a sample scenario,**
> **the meanings, and**
> **my attitudes when dealing with a child**

## How to Use My Word Patterns

As you read this book and apply my methods, keep in mind that you have to stay focused so you can use my word patterns correctly. I have that found not every child responds in the same way, but they all eventually understand I am in control and that seems to give them relief. You have to be aware of your child's personality when you apply these tools. I found it took a while for each child to trust that what I was doing would help and protect them. These word patterns and the way I show you to apply them will take some getting used to. A word about structure: structure is learning how to use and apply the correct word patterns to the correct situation and to keep repeating the same behavior every time your child does something wrong or right. As you apply your structure—and as you start to feel more comfortable with using these word patterns—this gets extremely easy and will empower you, so please be patient in the beginning.

In the beginning, the hardest part for me was to get past my anger. In time, as I became more aware of what was really going on within a child's mind, I just didn't feel angry anymore. So I do understand it will take some time for you to trust that what you are saying to your child will make a difference. It wasn't until I paid close attention to what I was saying to children and put that together with why children listened to me that I realized my words and actions really made a difference in each child's life.

I knew I had something special with the children; I just didn't know why. When I really thought about it, my answer was the words I used and the way I went about saying them. But more important, because I chose to apologize to a child when I scared them or comforted them when they became sad—by explaining to them why certain things were happening—they gave me something I call Respect. I knew I had something very few people have and that is the ability to win a child's heart by my actions and through the words I use. The reward I always got was that they listened to my words. So just know this will work, but you have to want it by making the effort it's going to take to obtain it.

> The word pattern, "Use Your Words," gives your child the opportunity to use his or her voice and is the backbone of every other word pattern I will give you.

## Sample Scenario

Bobby Manx always ran around the classroom hitting other kids and dumping over trash baskets and trashing things. One day, he hit the Coach.

The Coach stopped all activity. All the children looked at him. Usually bad things happened when a kid hit a teacher.

"Ouch. **That hurt my body**," the Coach said. He looked sadly at the dark-haired boy.

"Bobby, **I need you to use your words** and tell me why you did that!"

"Because you upset me!" Bobby said loudly. He looked mad.

"I'm sorry. I didn't mean to hurt your feelings. But we're not allowed to hit people. Is it okay if I hit you?" asked the Coach. All the kids looked wide-eyed at the Coach and Bobby.

"NO!" Bobby shouted.

"Why not? You hit me!" the Coach said. He still looked sad, not mean or mad.

"Because that would hurt me. I wouldn't like it," said Bobby. He looked sad, too.

"Do I have a happy face or a sad face?"

Bobby stood with his head down. He wouldn't look at the Coach.

The Coach repeated the question to the group.

"SAD FACE!" they yelled.

"It's because you hurt me! It **hurts my body when you hit me**! It makes me sad just like you! Ouch." The Coach made another sad face.

Bobby still wouldn't look at the Coach, but the Coach knelt on the floor next to him.

"Bobby, next time **I need you to use your words, not your hands** when something is bothering you or if I hurt your feelings! **Use your words** so that I can understand!"

Then the Coach stood up and looked at all of us. He was smiling.

"You don't have to be scared of me. I'm not going to hurt you! Just because I am talking loud doesn't mean I am trying to scare you! It means you scared me!

"If you don't want me to hit you then you are not allowed to hit me. It's only fair if you hit me I should be able to hit you, but I can't because we are not allowed to hit each other and this is why!"

"Bobby, do you want me to hit you?"

"No," Bobby answered, this time more quietly.

"I don't like it when you hit me! OKAY?" The Coach looked like he was waiting for Bobby to say something. "Say OKAY, Bobby!"

"Okay," said Bobby. He tried to look okay.

"I am sorry for hurting your feelings! I didn't mean to, and if I hurt your feelings again please **use your words and not your hands** to tell me when something is bothering you or if I upset you, OKAY?"

"OKAY," some of the children in the room shouted. And everyone laughed, even the Coach.

The Coach smiled and hugged Bobby quickly. Then he said, "**Thank you for using your words.** I like it when you talk to me. It helps me to understand what you want or need from me. Remember, if you don't tell me I won't know."

## Specific Word Patterns Make a Difference

I believe these specific word patterns will help you relate to your child and give him or her a voice. I believe if you use these word patterns in the way I am about to explain you will see the difference immediately. Children are the first to thank me for being nice or kind, and I believe it has to do with the words I use and the way I say them. I believe it is not me the children love but the way I talk to and protect them. I believe children understand I am protecting them as well as giving them a voice, and they respond to me in a way their parents have never seen. I would also add that I do repeat myself a lot when using these word patterns because you can use the same word pattern in a lot of different situations. Children find consistency in that. (When a child repeats an unacceptable behavior, I always respond by repeating the same word patterns for that behavior every time.) There are times when repeating yourself is good. This is one of those times. Also, you will see how one word pattern leads to another. These are the exact words you should get used to saying because your children will. Once you open this door, your children will hold you accountable because now they have the verbal tools to do just that; and when you forget, they will say these words right back to you. Trust me, it will happen, and you will hear something like "Mommy/Daddy, you're not listening to my words!"

I believe children are our future and we had better start helping them help us by learning how to communicate with them on a level they can understand. I also think it is important that you start to realize, as I educate you, the real problem: you think your child understands what you are trying to teach them through anger, threatening, and spanking. But I can assure you, once you see the light, you will change the way you talk, engage, and discipline your children for the rest of their lives.



## The Meanings of Word Patterns

It really helps if you ask your child to look at your face while talking to them; maybe you could get down on one knee. Making eye contact is important. Be kind in your approach because the purpose of these words is that you both (mainly you) can calm down and not get upset. These are learning tools and will help you be more consistent and predictable. If done correctly, your child will start to use these exact words and begin to hold you accountable.

Don't forget that each word pattern will fit every situation. You connect words like "want," "need," or "are feeling" and "I," "he," "she" to make the sentence complete. Example, "Use your words to tell me how you are feeling," or "I need you to use your words and tell me what you need."

USE YOUR WORDS—I say this word pattern religiously when I see a child scared, hurt, hurting someone or having a hard time communicating. In order to help a child I will say, "It's okay for you to talk to me. **Use your words** to tell me how you are feeling or what you want."



These words are meant to open the door to dialogue. I want the child to stop feeling scared or apprehensive and the only way I have found to do this successfully is to have the child **use their words.** I want children to tell me what they did right or wrong. I want them to start to learn though their own words what they did by telling me. When a child does something wrong and can't explain their actions, I have them repeat my words as I describe what they did. It's okay for you to give them the words. They need to learn the actual words to express themselves. I know **using their own words** helps children calm down so they can understand what they are doing instead of getting upset at you for yelling, threatening, or spanking them.

You can use this word pattern every time your child gives you a blank stare: "**Use your words to** tell me what's wrong." You help your child realize it's okay for them to tell you because you will keep them safe and help them say what's on their mind.

When you start to learn how your child thinks is when you will understand how much they don't know.

I also use this strategy when one child is bothering or hurting another child. When this happens, I stop everything and ask the child who is being hurt to **use your words** and tell the other child you don't like it when they do that and to please stop. When this happens, the child feels better because an adult stood up for them, but most of all they were able to tell the other child how they felt. See how that empowers a child. Children are extremely quick to **repeat words** when it helps to protect them. Giving children voices helps them to stand up for themselves.

**The word pattern "Use Your Words" gives your child the opportunity to use his or her voice and is the backbone of every other word pattern I will give you.**

Here are the sentences I use with this very important word pattern. Remember, keep it simple. I find when I say "I need you to…" I have a more serious tone, and when I say "use your words…" I have a softer tone.

- I need you to **use your words** and tell me why you…
- I need you to **use your words** and tell me what is bothering you.
- When I want something from you, I **use my words** and tell you.
- **Use your words** to tell me what you want.
- **Use your words, not your hands** to tell him how you feel or are feeling.
- When you **use your words,** it helps me to understand what you need from me.
- I like it when you **use your words and not your hands** or, Thank you for **using your words.**

Parents, there are many times you may have to give your child the words you want them to say, especially if they are having a hard time because they are frightened. It helps to keep in mind that children scare easily, so don't forget to apologize when you know they are scared. If someone else has hurt your child's feelings, use your words to remind your child how he feels so he can repeat those words to the child who has hurt him.

## Word Pattern Sequences

When children **use their words,** you must always say, "Thank you for **using your words!** I like that because it helps Mommy/Daddy to understand what you want, or need, or is bothering you!" A smile with a big hug goes a long way, and when they are real close and loving on you, tell them again: "I didn't mean to scare you but when you do . . . (describe what they did) that scares me, and I have to protect you. So don't forget; if you get hurt or don't listen to my words it scares me, or if you get in trouble I can get in trouble, too, because I am responsible for you." Ask them, "Do you want me to get in trouble?" When they answer "No," you have to say, "Then I need you to stop!"

This is what I call a word pattern sequence, and I will keep repeating this sequence the same way every time until a child understands, and when she does she will listen or stop the unacceptable behavior.

See how much information I have to give them? But trust me, as you get used to this way of thinking and talking, it gets extremely easy because the word pattern and sequences never change. It's always the same words, always the same reason, and always the same result. Your child is communicating with you as well as listening to your words!

## Word Patterns to Try

Following are examples of how I apply positive word patterns and why. Most of what I have learned came from how I said it. You may have already discovered that saying things with a positive outlook makes a world of difference.

Instead of a threat or command, use this word pattern:

**I NEED YOU TO LISTEN TO MY WORDS**

*or*

**YOU'RE NOT LISTENING TO MY WORDS**

This lets the child know you need them to stop what they are doing and pay attention. I use this to help children focus on what I am saying. I find when a child is not listening or I have to ask more than once, I will always say, "I need you to look at my face. I need you to listen to my words." Children relate to this word pattern well because it is simple; it should be used only with a calm voice. It also helps calm me down—and you.

Now this next word pattern should follow and can help show your child you listen to her words. When I lead by example, children respect me more and tend to respond to my words faster.

This is how I place an act back on the child:

I LISTEN TO YOUR WORDS WHEN YOU

ASK ME FOR SOMETHING

I say this word pattern only as a reference, *not for power*!

Parents, this one can't be toyed with. This is important because one of the reasons you have to ask your child over and over to do something goes back to how many times your child has to ask *you* for something. If you use this word pattern, it's important that when your child asks you, you answer right away or ask her to wait until you are finished; then, as soon as you can, apologize for making her wait and tell her you can now answer. This shows respect.

Making children ask more than once makes them feel sad and ignored, and that is why they turn the tables and make you ask. Because I "listen to your words," I seldom have to ask a child twice. Really! A few children will test to discover my reaction, and my reaction is always the same. I simply say, "I don't like repeating myself, do you?" Then I say, "How many times do you have to ask me when you want something?" Answer. "Once." (If they give me a different number, like eight, I know they are guessing.) For example, I will say, "How many times do I make you ask me for a stamp?" Then I will say, "I listen to your words, don't I?" Answer. "Yes." Then I will say, "I need you to listen to my words when I speak."

Notice how I always go back to how I treat them. This whole process is meant to show them how to listen and pay attention to you because you listen and pay attention to them. Remember, I am always going to ask you to be held accountable for your actions, as you should do with your child, by leading through example. If they have to ask twice, you will have to ask a lot more often than that.

If you have to keep asking your child to do something or for something, then this next word pattern is again leading by example. When I use this word pattern, it's unreal how many times children answer "ONCE!" I actually see the light go on over their heads and sometimes I even get a smile because I'm smiling. Then I give them a little hug and say, "Please stop making me ask so many times! It makes me sad." Then I hear, "Okay" or "Sorry, Coach."

If your child is not listening to your words, feel free to give them examples of when *you* listen to *their* words.

- "When you ask me to . . . I listen to your words. Yes or No." Then ask, "Do you know why?" If they answer, "No," say, "It's because I care about what you want or need." We want to help them if we can and using their words helps us to understand.

- "When you want me to . . . I listen to your words. Yes or No." Then ask, "Do you know why?" If they answer, "No," say, "I do it because it makes me happy when you let me do something for you or you ask for my help. When you use your words it helps me understand what you want."

- "When you need me to . . . I listen to your words. Yes or No." Then ask, "Do you know why?" If they answer, "No," say, "It's because I like being available to you. You count on me and by using your words I know what you want."

Then you must add, "So if you want me to listen to your words, I need you to listen to my words." Remember, if you do not get a good response the next time you have this conversation, you must let them know this is not acceptable and they are causing you to get involved.

Here is another word pattern I use to get my point across. I believe in placing the act back on the children because it helps them realize what they are doing.

I DON'T LIKE REPEATING MYSELF, DO YOU?
HOW MANY TIMES
DO I MAKE YOU ASK ME FOR SOMETHING?

Don't make them ask more than once. If you do, **don't** use this word pattern! This is used only to show them you don't make them ask more than once.

I am very careful when I say this because I use this word pattern as a learning tool, not out of anger, frustration or for power. When I use this word pattern, I am trying to show the child that I listen to their words and that they would not like it if they had to keep asking me over and over when they wanted something. This is a perfect way for you to lead by example. When I say this word pattern, children know I don't make them ask more than once, and when they test this issue, I will make them ask over and over and over when they want something from me. After they realize I am ignoring them, I immediately tell them why I made them ask so many times. This will help them start to learn about other people's feelings. I only do this when a child is testing me. Placing feeling back onto children is the best way for them to understand other people have feelings, too. "How do you like it when…" or "How would you like it if…" is a great way to start off these types of sentences.

Now after I say this, I will tell them why and my answer is always the same: "It hurts my feelings or makes me sad when I have to ask you so many times." Then I will ask, "How does it make you feel when you have to ask over and over when you want something from me?" I find I do ask the children, "Why are you acting in this way?"; I do tell them, "I am doing this because …"; and I do ask, "How does that make you feel?" all the time!

Parents, you must change the way you communicate with your child. Move away from the aggressive, threatening command and toward these word patterns that allow children to tell you in their own words why they acted in a certain way. I never use aggression or threats and I am rewarded *for not doing so.*

These word patterns are for when you want to talk about feelings.

HOW DOES/DID THAT MAKE YOU FEEL?

I say this word pattern when I or someone else does something to a child they don't like because it allows the child to describe feelings. You must use this word pattern in your child's daily life. If a child hurts you or someone else, please have a kind heart, control your facial expressions, and use a serious tone! Remember, angry facial expressions can cause your child to become scared and hear something completely different from the point you're trying to make.

I talk to children about their feelings a lot in the beginning because children relate to their feelings first. I will remember what the child is saying about how it makes them feel so that I can remind them in later conversations. Also, asking this question allows me to introduce children to the fact that I, and other people, have feelings, too.

For example, say your child said or did something to you that you didn't like. It will help your child understand the value of someone else's feelings if you say, "How would you like it if I said or did that to you?" Most of the time the child will tell you it would make them sad or they wouldn't like it. That's when you say, "When you . . . (describe what the child did), that hurts my feelings, too." Children under the age of five cannot totally grasp what the word "feelings" means. (If you don't believe me, ask them!) They do not understand anything except how *they* feel or how *they* are being treated.

I find most children learn faster if they can feel it for themselves and not just through words. If you use this word pattern, it will help your child understand there are boundaries. Having things placed back on your child is a great way for anyone to learn that the world is not all about them. After you say this word pattern, the very next one is always . . .

WOULD YOU LIKE IT IF I/HE/SHE DID THAT TO YOU?<br>THAT'S WHY YOU ARE NOT ALLOWED<br>TO DO THAT TO ME/THEM

Placing the value of what they did back onto them is the best way for your child to understand what you're talking about. (I keep repeating certain things because, as I said, my thought process and the words I use stay the same even when the situation or scenario changes.) This will take time for them to understand. This word pattern should be used when your child is hurting you or someone else. Helping your child start to understand about feelings is a great way for you to help them become less selfish. Now if your child hurts you your next word pattern will be . . .

**LOOK AT MY/HIS/HER FACE.**

**DO I OR DOES HE/SHE HAVE A HAPPY FACE OR SAD FACE?**

Children need to see others' pain or sadness to understand that other people have feelings. Remember, children read facial expressions. Letting them see what they did to me/another child and how that made me/them feel is extremely important because nowadays children just say "I'm sorry" and think everything is okay. Having your child see another child's emotions should be the way adults deal with their child. Having them look at a child's face and seeing the pain still isn't enough.

Explain to your child that to say sorry but not feel sorry is not appropriate. We should defend the other child. Ask your child if the person he hurt can turn around and hurt him, and when your child answers "No," ask, "Why not?" "Why not?" is the correct way to show your child why we don't hurt others. Answer: because we don't want it done to us. Sometimes I will ask the other child if they want to do it back to them and when the child answers "Yes," you should see the look on your child's face. Fear. Once I have asked this, I explain to the hurt child, "We are not allowed to hurt others," then I look at the other child and say to him, "See, I wouldn't let them do that to you, so I can't let you do that to them."

Sometimes I use the word *protect*. This is a great way to show your child you will protect them, and that it is not appropriate to hurt someone else.

This is a tricky one. The child has to be old enough to be able to empathize. Telling a child that something they just did or said has hurt your feelings doesn't do any good unless you tell them why. "I am sorry" doesn't help because they don't understand how to feel what the other person feels. You can let them feel what you mean through role-playing (role-playing for me is when I explain each child's action). If you want your child to understand you when you say this, they first have to live it. Using the word pattern How Does That Make You Feel is a great way to do this. Explaining feelings can only be done if you place the value back on your child. For example, after I say, "That hurt my feelings!" I say, "Is it okay if I do that to you?" The child answers, "No!" Then I ask, "Why not?" and he answers, "Because I wouldn't like that," or "It would make me sad." That's when I can introduce my feelings by saying, "That hurts my feelings when you do that to me!" Then lastly, I will let the child see me being sad. (Be careful if your child gets sad because most of the time, believe it or not, they are still thinking you are being mean to them.)

### IT MAKES ME SAD WHEN YOU HURT MY FEELINGS

It is important for you to tell your child when they make you sad or hurt your feelings. Letting them see you sad is okay. Notice I didn't say angry. Controlling your feelings will show them how to recover when they are sad. Remember parents, having your feelings hurt and being mad are not the same things to children. When you get mad, you just scare your child. Telling your child they made you sad can cause your child to cry or be sad, but I can assure you in their minds they are still thinking they did something wrong and you are mad at them. You must take a gentler approach if you want your child to understand you are sad because of something they did. Telling them they hurt your feelings is a much better way to communicate with them. Anger doesn't work. Talking to a child from a learning aspect is a way I find to be better for them. When you are addressing your feelings, you have to be very careful if you want your child to really understand what you mean.

———

YOU SCARED ME OR YOUR BODY IS SCARING ME

(their actions)

It is okay to let children know they are scaring you or that their actions scared you. Remember, everything we are trying to communicate to the child should go back to the fact that you are responsible for them.

I find if you let the child know why you are upset, it will go a long way in helping them know right from wrong, but it has to be done carefully. I get the best result when I say, "You are scaring me," or "Your body scared me," and "I have to protect you," and "If you get in trouble, I get in trouble." Letting a child know you are responsible for them gives them security. Children know the words "get in trouble". If a child knows you can get in trouble for their actions it will help them behave better because they don't want you to get in trouble. When I tell a child they are scaring me, they don't think I am angry or upset. Later, it catches their attention. It's like they hear a word they can relate to! I see it in their eyes and in the way they respond to that phrase.

Here are some of the word patterns I use when a child scared me or is scaring me:

- Jonathan, you are scaring me, or Jonathan, your body scared me.
- Katy, when you don't pay attention to my words, it scares me.
- Sally, I need you to tell Bobby to use his words, not his hands.
- Jonathan, do you like it when I scare you?

- Katy, I need you to control your body on the balance beam, you are scaring me.
- Jonathan, when you act silly on the balance beam it scares me.

### THIS IS MY BODY

One of the first things I talk about when I am with children is their bodies. Children need to learn that their body is not to be touched by other people or children and that their arms, legs, heads, etc., are their body. I use the word "body" every time I want them to address themselves. This is another great word when you want your child to check themselves. You can say, "I need you to check your body," or "Do you need to check your body?" This can also be applied when it comes to bathroom issues. This word pattern also helps direct the child's mind to their body as the reason why I am getting involved, rather than think I am being mean. It helps them to better relate to the situation I find.

### THIS IS MY BODY AND YOU ARE
### NOT ALLOWED TO TOUCH ME

I teach this to children by having them repeat it after me. I say this word pattern, and they repeat it when a child hurts or touches them when they didn't want them to. I value this word pattern for many reasons. Children need to learn that it is **not** okay for anyone to touch them, especially if they don't want them to. This word pattern is very empowering to a child. I also encourage children to tell me when someone hurts their body so I can say, "You are not allowed to touch their body. That hurts them." When a child sees a parent standing up for them it lets them know it is okay for them to say it. And they will.

### CONTROL YOUR BODY

Because I am now using the word "body," the child starts to become familiar with what it means, allowing me to use that as a catalyst.

It also allows me to introduce the word "control" and explain what that means. This is a great word pattern to use when you feel your child is out of control. It will help you not to scream, threaten or spank because now you can give control back to them for what they did or are doing. You can do this by saying . . .

CONTROL YOUR BODY OR I WILL HAVE TO

- I need you to control your body.
- If you can't control your body I will have to.
- If you can't control your body you will have to walk away.
- Since you can't control your body I need you to walk away.
- Your body is scaring me.
- I need you to walk away (or just walk away).

I say this before I take any action in order to give the child a chance to walk away or correct their actions before I get involved. I only say this once and they know it. I never break this rule. This does not apply when a child is hurting another child. Walking away is the punishment. I find this works well.

WALK AWAY

This is one of my favorites because it doesn't allow my feelings to get involved. This word pattern works extremely well because it is simple and children seem to understand the meaning. I also like this because it allows the child to get a second chance sooner rather than later. Plus, it is a kinder way to handle an out-of-control situation. Rather than punishing a child with time-out or missing a turn, I simply say, "Because you cannot control your body, I need you to walk away."

Remember, when a child is told to walk away, they are upset at having to walk away, and also at you. This is a great time for you to ask your child if they know why they were asked to walk away, as well as for you to start to see how your child thinks and how what you thought you were teaching and accomplishing wasn't getting accomplished at all. In fact, the opposite was happening: your child was getting upset at everything and everyone except themselves.

Curious how that is, but, as you now know it is a normal behavior for all children because they are scared or intimidated by what you are doing and saying to them. I understand why some parents think their child understands their aggressive behavior when the parents try to correct them: it's because of the child's reaction, like cowering down, or demonstrating remorse by showing a sad face or crying because they are realizing what they did was wrong. I understand these parents are using words that they feel work because they are getting a payoff for it by hurting their child because the child has hurt the parent. I get it; I used to think the same way. When a child showed me these kinds of behaviors when I scolded them, it made me believe they understood.

But please, no. I have learned through trial and error how this way of thinking has never got anyone where they want to go. This is why: the child has never understood your way of thinking or your meaning. So keep in mind, if the child walks away without knowing why they are being punished or what they did, they will feel sad, frustrated, and sorry for themselves. That's why I will let the child know that if they don't like walking away, they must correct their behavior. When they do I will let them join the group activity or area.

So keep in mind that for a child, the apology and hug during this time will make all the difference. And please remember, just because you apologize or hug does not mean you are accepting their behavior. You are being a responsible parent who wants to show your child patience and understanding through example.

## YOU CAN HURT YOUR BODY

I like talking about safety. Here are two more examples of that. First, let them know they could hurt their body. I think it is important to tell a child to be careful when they are playing. I ask the children to repeat this phrase: "Gymnastics is not supposed to hurt my body. If it does, it means I did something wrong. Tell Coach and he will show me what I did wrong so it won't hurt my body." I also teach them to say, "Coach wants to make sure I'm okay. Gymnastics is supposed to be fun. It's not supposed to hurt my body." (I will repeat this every time before class.)

As I learn more about the brain I have discovered that children must first learn from experience. It's the experience that teaches our children, not so much the words; but I find if you explain about safety and what that means, it helps the child predict what will or might happen, just as I've noted about other behaviors. Letting a child know they can **hurt their bodies** will help if done with meaning through explanation. Parents, don't forget, children unfortunately need to learn the hard way most of the time. It's a part of our learning life. If talked about correctly you can use this as a catalyst for trusting you. For example, you could say, "I told you that **you could hurt your body**," or "If you're not careful, you will **hurt your body!**"

Parents, here is something you should be aware of: often when children hurt themselves and I ask, "Are you okay?" they will say "Yes" when I can clearly tell they are not. In these situations, I tell a child, "It's okay to say, 'No, I hurt my leg/arm/head.'" Then I will address their pain. While doing this, I will ask them to repeat my words: "Say, 'I hurt my leg/arm/head.'" Then I say, "It's okay to tell me when you hurt your body. I need to know so I can make sure you're okay." I go back to the very first word pattern I used with them—the one I've been teaching you in this book: I say, "Don't be scared to **use your words** when you get hurt." I want to reassure them I need to know. Most kids think that if they get hurt, they will get in trouble. Because of their fear, I find I have to pay attention to a child's face, body, and movement before I believe they are okay.

> I find I ask the children all the time, "Why are you acting in this way?" Then I tell them, "I am doing this because . . ." followed by, "How does that make you feel?"

Even after I tell children they could get hurt or could hurt their bodies in gymnastics, when I ask them, "Could you get hurt in here?" they still answer "No." Play can lead to falling down and getting hurt, so when they answer "No" it's because they are guessing.

You will notice that they can't make the connection because they can't reason. Children under the age of six really need your patience when it comes to understanding. I find most children have to live the experience first. Then, with proper communication and over time, they can relate the words to an action.



I talk a lot about safety space. I use this word pattern to let children know to pay attention to the things around them. Learning how to wait their turn or not crash into the person in front of them is difficult for some children. I find children become absorbed in the moment and when this happens your child will get hurt. Having your child slow down and think before they react is a great way to help them pay attention. I teach about safety space by making the children cautious of their bodies. In my class, if a child accidentally hits someone, it was his fault and he must take a break and sit out. During this break, I explain why each person waits for a turn and tell them to watch and learn how everyone else waits for their turn. (I do this kindly.) I will talk about **the space between students** and tell them this is their **safety space**. As long as there is space between children, no one will get hurt. I will ask the children to repeat the words **Safety Space** before we start each class and continue to have them repeat me while class is going on. Again, having the children repeating my words while they are doing something, I find, helps them to remember what is being asked of them.

## More Word Patterns to Try

I use words like the following because they are a gentler way of saying the old-school phrases (like "I told you to stop," "Wait," "If you don't quit," "I said no," etc.). You may still think the only way your child can learn is if you are aggressive with them, but now you are choosing to handle it in a different way, new-school. Remember, when a child thinks you are yelling at them or threatening them, they respond negatively. I find when I use words like the following, I get a better result.

- I need you to calm down.
- Please! Don't hurt . . . be gentle.
- I need you to be patient.
- Do I need to get involved?
- I need you to slow down.
- Your body is scaring me.
- Do you need my help?
- You are not listening to my words.
- Remember, you could hurt your body.
- I need you to use your words, not your hands.
- I didn't mean to scare you.
- I have asked nicely twice. If I have to ask again, I am going to be upset.
- Do you need a hug?

Try to come up with some of them on your own.

These word patterns are truly amazing. As you engage your child, he will start telling you everything you want to know with these words. Engaging your child with word patterns like these will teach you about your child through the words you both use because you are now learning together.

These word patterns are meant for this exact purpose so you can lead by example as well as hold your child accountable for their actions. Plus, these patterns teach you both about life through communication—another way of handling things besides yelling, threatening, or spanking. This type of engagement has been a beautiful thing for me.

## My Attitude as I Work With Children

The following sentences and phrases come from a different perspective: they are what I say to myself as I'm working with children.

These words didn't just come to me. As I observed over one hundred teachers, I learned what concepts, words, and actions worked to keep children safe and moving forward. These statements are the foundations for my approach to the children in my care.

I've been saying them so long, they are always in my mind. Why? Because they help me stay calm, remind me what I'm doing, why I'm doing it, and that it's the right thing to be doing.

You may want to make flashcards or sticky notes of the affirmations to put around your house to keep reminding you that you're the parent, you're doing the right thing, and, maybe most important, they take a lot of the guesswork out of a situation.

**I always protect children from each other and they know it because I give them a voice.** Allow children to use their own words to protect themselves from others. When children know the right words to use, they will use them every time. Children are empowered when they can tell others they are not allowed to hurt them.

**I always pay attention to them when they first ask. I rarely make them ask more than once, and if I do, I apologize.** When children don't believe that I'll pay attention, they misbehave. When children finally understand that I always pay attention, they like me for it. My word patterns work because I am held accountable and have a kind attitude.

**I always let them know they could get hurt** (in my class, but it might be on a playground or at a friend's house). **Why do I want to know? So I can tell them what they did wrong—so they don't do it again—as well as so I can comfort them.** I find it important to ask each child whether they know why I am asking or doing something. Then you know whether they understand your words and that you can believe what they tell you.

**I always tell a child it is okay for him to tell me something even if he doesn't want to or thinks he might get in trouble.** Children must learn to trust you. I find when a child gets hurt, they sometimes feel they can get in trouble if they tell you.

**I always tell them they are doing a good job and that I am proud of them.** Engagement—this will help to increase their confidence and self-esteem. This will also help connect you with your child. Children love sincere praise.

**I let them see me smile. I tell them they make me smile.** Letting your children see you happy is *always* a good thing; it shows them you notice and approve of what they are doing.

**I always give them lots of choices.** Punishment is not always the answer. Give them another chance. Choices are how I determine if I can trust a child. Allowing children to make choices shows me a lot about their personalities because their choices reveal consequences.

**I always hold them accountable.** That doesn't always mean punishment. When I lead by example, I pay attention because I am held accountable, which in turn allows me to hold each child accountable. My main objective is to get the child to communicate with me so I understand them better. That way I can determine how to handle the situation.

**I never punish through anger.** Remember, aggression toward your child makes him either shut down or become aggressive himself and the situation may escalate. When you calm down, you can use explanation and child's currency

**I know children like to experiment. I try to remember that they are not out to hurt me. They are doing the best they can with what they have.** I am the adult. When your child is having a hard day, being mischievous, or experimenting, this is your opportunity to shine, to teach, to be the adult. This isn't about you, remember, it's about their feelings. Hugs are highly recommended.

**Most children will test to find their boundaries.** Children learn through testing you, and knowing that allows you to approach things in a different way. The child is still learning and you are their teacher. Remember, children are not small adults.

**Don't forget that children do not understand the concept of time until age eight or nine.** Please try not to use this concept with young children. Remember five minutes is five hours, and they don't get it. Giving your child even a moment out will teach him or her something. Punishing too long gives me a different result after the punishment.

**It is easy to hurt a child's feelings.** If you fail to acknowledge and apologize for hurting a child's feelings, they will stop paying attention. Give *them* respect and they will repay you by paying attention to you and giving you a lot of respect. This will happen if you give them a second chance sooner rather than later.

**Just remember, when you punish a child they are not thinking "my bad"; they get scared and angry.** Knowing this, I try not to get angry. I remember that I need to do a better job with explaining, having patience and, most of all, being compassionate. Remember, this is normal behavior for all children. I must get past this for anything to work or make sense to me.

**Children live their world in their mind. Me, Me, or I, I.** This is a normal way of thinking for a child under the age of three or four. Children slowly learn about others' feelings. You have

to introduce this to them.  You cannot force this upon them.
A child should be able to be a child. This only lasts for a short
period of time so if you can appreciate this time in your
child's life, it will make a huge difference for you.

## Positive Word Patterns I Use

I say these words with positive tones, positive facial expressions,
and passion. Below you will find more examples or ideas of how to go
about using your words.

**Look at my face.** I'll point at my face and smile big. This helps a
child make eye contact and see I am proud of them.

**You make me smile!** Children like to see my expressions and love to
get compliments. It helps break the ice and encourage new
students.

**I am proud of you!** I let them know they made a good decision.

**Good for you!** or **Good job!** It lets them know you noticed and liked
their effort. Praise gives them a greater feeling of self-worth.

**I'm going to tell your Mom!** I am. I'm going to tell her you listened to
my words! I say this because it lets me see the child think, and
it helps me to know which child listens to *tones* and reads *facial
expressions* and which child listens and understands my *words*.

**You listened to my words! Thank you!** This pattern makes the child
aware that he was listening and gives him an idea of what
listening is. I say this a lot when I am trying to teach a child a
phrase, especially if they are having a hard time or a hard day
with their behavior.

**You were watching! Good for you!** It highlights for them that I
noticed they were paying attention and that they are learning
how to pay attention. I want to give positive feedback to a
child at the moment they're doing the action they have the
most trouble doing. This is the best way to teach it!

**High Five!** I mainly do this for kids who are hesitant when they get
around me. It gives them an opportunity to connect with me
in a quick and easy-going way. Plus, it's a fun way to give
praise to all the children.

**Trust Coach Bruce!** I use the word "trust" a lot. Here are some
examples: I have them repeat, "Trust Coach Bruce; he won't
let me fall," as long as I am helping; or "I can help you if you
trust that I won't let you fall or get hurt": or "Thank you for
trusting me. See, I didn't let you fall or get hurt."

**Sing a child's song.** This helps the children calm down and they like
it. I also do this because I want the children to get used to
hearing my voice while they are focused on what they are
doing. It teaches them to listen while they are occupied, helps
soothe them and relate to me because they've heard these
songs at home.

- Twinkle, Twinkle Little Star
- You Are My Sunshine
- A Barney Song: I Love You, You Love Me®

Repeat well-known sayings from children's cartoons or books.
This relates me to the child and opens the door for them to
communicate with me.
Examples:

- You So Totally Rock, Dude! (*Finding Nemo*®)
- You Rock

- That Was Totally Righteous
- To Infinity and Beyond! *(Toy Story®)*

I give them choices, lots of choices. (Choices are how a child feels in control. Because it is their choice it allows me to hold them accountable for that choice. Choices are how I let a child become an individual.)

Example:

- Show me the skill you like most!
- Choice of what they want to do. (Free turn)
- If they would like a stamp or not.

I give them the choice of whether to do it or not. If they don't want to do a skill they don't have to. All they have to say is, "I don't want to do that." and I say, "Okay." As they pass I say, "High Five" or "Thank you for using your words," or "If you ever want to try, let me know and I will help you. I promise I won't let you fall."

---

# What Should I Do When . . .

Now you have learned the Word Patterns that make The Power so helpful, appropriate, and workable. To put them to use requires time and practice and you know your child will give you both! What follows are answers to some of the most common questions parents have asked me, the reasoning behind my answers and, most important, *the words to use*. Please remember, I've taught thousands of children and learned through more trial and error than most parents get in a lifetime. I don't mean to say that these are the only answers, but they are a good place to start working with your child.

**1. Why do I have to keep asking my child to do something?**

> **Answer:** This stems from two things. First: when they ask you a question and you don't answer them the first time, you are teaching them how to ignore you. Second, you are not consistent in your discipline because your child is not worried about the outcome. Answer them the first time they ask and use that as your reason not to allow them to ignore *you* when you ask. If you make a mistake and they have to ask you more than twice, apologize immediately, then answer their question or problem.

**What I do:** This is a time for you to show patience and love by placing the value of what your child is doing back on them by explaining why you don't make them ask over and over when they want something from you.

**What I say:** The first thing you must do is use my word patterns like this! This is the sequence I will follow every time a child is not listening to my words.

1. Tell them they are not listening to your words.
2. Ask them, "Do I listen to your words when you ask me a question or for something?"
   **(Sorry you don't get to use this one yet; you have to earn it!)**
3. Ask them, "How many times do you have to ask me for something?"
   **(Be careful with this one. You better only make them ask you once.)**
4. Tell them, "I need you to listen to me when I ask you a question or for something."
   **(Sorry you don't get to use this one yet; you have to earn it!)**
5. Tell them the reason why you want them to listen.
   **(Be specific.)**
6. Tell them if you have to ask again, they will lose something they like. **(Child's Currency.)**
7. Tell them this is not an option. Repeating yourself with kind words and/or maybe even helping them with what you are asking them to do is a kind gesture. This goes a long way toward showing your child you care.
8. If they have to be punished, tell them you cannot reward bad behavior; and if they don't want to continue to lose the things they like, then it is important that they respond when you ask them the first time.

## 2. What should I do and say when my child lies to me?

**Answer:** This behavior stems from your child being scared you are going to spank or ground them. They don't trust you. I find children lie because parents discipline them in a mean way, are not consistent with discipline, or make rash promises that are not kept. And your child lies to test your parenting skills. (When your child tests your parenting skills, it tells me you aren't consistent or fair.) I also find that when a child doesn't fear me, they will tell me.

**What I do:** This is a time for you to explain to your child why we don't lie. Asking them questions about how it makes them feel when someone lies to them is a great way to start. Explaining to children that lying is a bad thing as well as explaining why we don't lie to others will help. I find the more I can make a child feel what I am saying the more it helps them to understand lying is unacceptable.

**What I say:** This is how I approach a child when they lie to me. This is the sequence I will follow every time a child lies to me.

1.  I will start by telling myself to be gentle in my approach because I know if I get aggressive the child is going to lie to me. I say, "I need you to use your words and tell me if you did…"
2.  Before they answer, I say, "Remember, you do not need to be scared of me. I'm only asking because I need to know. If you tell me, then I can explain why I need you not to do that." I do this to keep reassuring them it is okay to talk with me.
3.  Then I always tell the child I am responsible for them and I can get in trouble if I don't correct them. I find this seems to take away some of their fear.

4. I will also add that telling me doesn't mean they will get in trouble. I find if the child is willing to talk and is listening to my words as I correct them that is all I will ask of them. Sometimes talking and sharing information is enough. Remember, my attitude is to teach rather than scold.

5. Then I will say, "Thank you for using your words and telling me that you did…" If the situation calls for discipline, use child's currency and remind them you cannot reward bad behavior or lying.

6. During this conversation you must ask them if it is okay for you to lie to them. Ask them how it makes them feel when someone lies to them. In these situations, you must use an example of when someone lied to them so as to place the feeling of how they felt when it was done to them. Children learn faster when they can feel it for themselves.

7. If a child continues to lie, I tell them they are telling me I cannot trust them, and if that is the case, they are no longer allowed to play with me. I tell them this is because they are now scaring me, and I am going to get in trouble. When this happens, the child loses all their privileges with me and has to earn them back by being honest when they do something.

In these situations the main objective is to let the child know they can trust you and not fear you. If you ever want this to change, you have to be willing to handle it with care and understanding, not anger or frustration. If you do, then just know your child feels the same way you do: frustrated, angry, and upset.

I can proudly say children very seldom lie to me. When they do, I test their answer through talking.

**3. What should I do and say when my child throws a temper tantrum?**

**Answer:** This is happening because you have not discussed the word NO and why you are saying it. The love you have for your child and wanting them to have the things you didn't has caused part of this. The other part stems from your not knowing what to do when your child reacted with a tantrum, so you finally gave to your screaming, out-of-control child what they wanted so they would stop.

**What I do:** I find there are a couple ways to handle a tantrum, but first you must understand what is causing your child to do this. Only then will you understand what you have to do in order to correct it. In case you don't know, tantrums stem from selfish reasons. Children act out in this way because you are not giving them what they want when they want it. Your child is very upset and does not understand why you are denying them what they want. In other words, your child is trying to run the household.

Okay, now you have to do whatever it takes to calm your child down. I do this by having a calm demeanor and not acknowledging the child's behavior. I use polite words and keep reassuring the child everything is going to be okay, and they do not have to be upset. I try to make this as loving as I can. I want to show only calm behavior because I know if I don't it is only going to make matters worse. Try picking up your child and holding them until they stop crying. You can shush them and tell them you love them. (Parents, please do not give your child what they are asking for.) Once your child is calm, then explain why you are telling them no. Being aggressive or putting a child who is in this state in time-out is not acceptable.

**What I say:** Here are some ideas that worked for me. This is the sequence I will follow every time a child throws a temper tantrum.

1.  I tell them, "This behavior is unacceptable and I need you to control your body."

2.  I tell them, "If you don't calm down and stop crying, you are going to get sick." (Vomit.) Do not acknowledge their behavior.

3.  I say, "Use your words and tell me why you are upset."

4.  After they say, "Because you're not giving or doing what I want," I tell them why I can't. ("Because I told you so" is not acceptable.)

5.  I tell children "I am the adult and the reason I am not doing what you want is because…."

6.  I tell the child, "I am sorry you are sad but now is not the time for you."

7.  I ask them, "How would it make you feel if I just started crying and getting upset when you told me no?" (Remember, it will always help a child if they can feel what you mean.)

8.  If I have to control the child's body there is a different approach I take. This approach will only be taught in my seminars or at lectures. It is too difficult to explain and must be seen in order to have its full intention displayed. Trust me when I say that if I have to get involved the temper tantrum never happens again, and it only takes me getting involved once. (I learned this from Carla. It works and I have applied this method to several students, with amazing results.)

9.  Once I get the child calm, my main goal is always to let the child know I wasn't being mean, and just because I said no doesn't mean they were bad or I don't like them. It just means they can't have it right now.

10. I always tell the child the real reason so they know. Even if they won't understand it will help them the next time this comes up. It will allow me to refer to this moment again in the future.

11. Having building blocks like this so you can refer to them later will always help you to help your child understand what you mean even when they can't. It's a building block!

12. I find the more honest and consistent I am, the less this happens as long as I keep repeating this type of behavior every time they have a tantrum.

13. If I have to use child's currency, it's always after the fact, when the child is calm. I always remind them I cannot reward bad behavior. Once your child understands you are committed and have a plan that stays the same, things like this will most definitely stop happening.

14. I also find if the child can correct themselves during this conversation, there is no discipline. Remember, my attitude is to teach rather than to scold. Use your building blocks; remind them of past experiences.

Parents, please keep in mind when your child has a temper tantrum, that it's the time for you to shine by helping your child break this habit.

## 4. How can I stop this from happening?

**Answer:** I find I need to let children know what I am doing and why I do it to keep things like this from happening. The more I talk about the word "no" in our daily life, the more a child is likely not to get upset when I tell them no. If I explain to the child beforehand the reasons why I have to tell them no, it helps them deal with it better when I do say no. If I role-play with the word "no," it also helps a lot. In our regular time together, I ask questions like "Do you know why when we go to the . . . and you ask me for . . . have to say no?" I will also tell children I don't like telling them no, but we can't always have what we want. Sometimes I will make references to things I want that I can't have. Remember, asking questions and involving your child in your daily life will help them to relate to you better and will help with testing and behavioral issues.

**5. What should I do and say when I know I've hurt my child's feelings?**

**Answer:** I find it is easy to hurt a child's feelings. Sometimes I do so just by correcting them when they do something wrong as well as by making promises that I don't or cannot keep.

I find this is important to me because children remember. They live in their minds and because they do, they can feel sorry for themselves quickly. This is one of the reasons I think it is important for me to apologize and tell a child when I make mistakes. Teaching children how to forgive at an early age is important to their social development.

**What I do:** When I know I have made a child sad, I will ask them to use their words and tell me what I did that made them sad. Once they tell me, no matter what their answer is, I will apologize for making them sad and tell them I did not mean to hurt their feelings. (After that, if they did something wrong, I will say, "It was because you scared me and I have to protect you.") Then I will give the child a hug and tell them if they don't want me to make them sad then they need to stop doing what they did. I will thank them for using their words and telling me I made them sad and will remind them that if they don't use their words I won't know.

**What I say:** I think it is important that you acknowledge your child's words by telling the child to "use their words" so you can understand what the problem is.

1.  Addressing their sadness is hugely important.
2.  Use your words and ask them if there is anything you can do for them. Offering them a hug as comfort is always nice.
3.  If your child is sad because of something you did, then use your words and tell the child you didn't mean to hurt their feelings.

4.  When you use your words to explain to the child the reason you made them sad, you connect with your child. It helps you to show them respect.

5.  When you make your child sad, I find just listening to what they have to say and addressing their pain goes a long way toward helping your child learn how to forgive you and others. I believe children want to be heard, and when I listened, I learned.

6.  Now, if you hurt your child's feelings because you had to protect the child, then use your words and explain that reason to the child. Tell them if they want you to stop, then they must correct their behavior.

7.  If you have to discipline, use your words and explain to the child you cannot reward bad behavior. I keep saying this because it's a softer way of saying, "You were bad, now you're in trouble," or "I'm going to tell your father." Don't forget, if you talk down to your child when you correct them they become sad. Using your words to explain to the child why you did or are doing something is being a parent and talking like this is highly recommended.

**6. What should I do and say when I know my child is sad or needs my help with something?**

**Answer:** These are the moments I cherish the most because this is my opportunity to teach or help. In these moments is your opportunity to teach your child how to communicate with you as well as how to ask for help. Remember, my goal is to have the child be the one to ask me for help or to tell me they are sad and why. In my world, I find that with most children I don't even have to ask because as soon as a child becomes sad at something or someone, they tell me. It's funny how this works. I find that after children trust me as an adult I don't have any issues with sadness or the lack of ability to help a child. I also find that having children repeat some of my words in our daily life helps them to use those words in times of difficulty.

**What I do:** I always ask them to use their words and tell me why they are sad. When it comes to help, I will say, "If you want me to help you, you have to use your words and tell me what you need." In either case, my intentions are always to get the child to tell me with their words.

**What I say when I see a child sad:** Here are some ideas that worked for me.

Noticing your child is sad is very important because it gives you an opportunity to use your words and explain to your child how to use their words. I find when a child is sad they are very vulnerable and can be directed easily.

1. When a child is sad in my class I will let them know I don't like it when they are sad because it makes me sad. It makes me sad because I love them.
2. Then I will ask them to use their words and tell me why they are sad. If they are sad with me and I know it, I will help them by saying what I think may be on their mind. Then I ask them to repeat those words in order to help them feel comfortable with telling me how they feel.
3. When they tell me, it gives me a chance to show them love and comfort, so I will usually ask them if they need a hug. After engaging, I find through our talk I can help them with their sadness. Sometimes they just needed a hug or someone to pay attention to them.

**What I say when I see a child needs my help:** Recognizing a child needs help is very important to them because that's how I allow children to feel safe in my environment. Because safety and help are so important to me, I realize how careful I have to be with each situation. I say each situation because in these cases you have to allow the child to take the lead by asking for your help or being available when they need it.

1.  Asking children if you can help rather than saying you will help is the best way to approach children. I have also discovered I will have children repeat words like "Help me, Coach" as a part of our everyday class because I want my children to feel comfortable saying those words.
2.  I say things like "If you need my help say, 'Help me, Coach' and I will help you." Under certain circumstances, I say, "Can I help you?" or "Do you need my help?" I find giving the child the chance to decide if they really want your help or if they are just testing to see what you might do is just another way for a child to see if they can trust you.
3.  I find most of the time a child needs help with something only once or twice. If they keep asking, it's because they are testing to see what you are going to do or say. If a child really needs help, I can tell by the situation and can address it accordingly. Don't forget, when it comes to things outside the classroom, I believe children will and can learn faster if they do it by themselves, but guidance and supervision are always highly recommended.

**7. What should I do and say when I cannot help them or give them the time I need to because I have to work?**

**Answer:** I feel for so many parents in this predicament. The best answer I can give you is to ask a lot of questions and to check on their schoolwork. Doing these two things will help your child feel that you are interested and want to be involved.

Have conversations about why you have to work. Explain why you cannot be more involved. Tell them you wish you could be more involved and be supportive in other ways: ask numerous questions about what they did in and out of school; ask questions about how they think they did on tests or in competitions or sports, or why they are interested in something.

**What I do:** This is another opportunity for you to engage with your child by talking to them about what they do each day. Try to be helpful with things they may be having difficulty with, but most of all you have to make time for them and their schoolwork whenever you can. I know it's rough, but even if you don't know how to answer your child, at least try to work out the problem together. (If you're not able to help your child with schoolwork, you might find someone who can tutor your child. Call a local university or high school or find out if your child's school offers a student or teacher tutoring program.)

**What I say:** Here are ideas I tried when a child would tell me they missed their parent, or would cry for mommy or daddy, or sometimes would ask me where their parents were.

1. First, I would tell them I could tell they were sad or that something was bothering them.
2. I would ask why and was there anything I could do to make them feel better.
3. When a child said that he felt sad because his parents worked, I explained that it was because they have to pay bills so they could have clothes, go to school, buy food, and have a home. I tell the child it's the same as having to go to school. Everyone has to go to school; it's the law. Mommy or Daddy has to go to work so they can pay the bills and take care of you. It's the law. It's how

adults have to do it. I also tell them that if it were up to Mommy or Daddy, they would rather be home spending their time with you. You can say these same things to your children. You can point out things your family needs and likes and tell them that everyone has a job so the whole family can enjoy those things. (You don't want them to feel guilty that they must "work" in order to eat, but it's okay for them to feel part of the family in this way.) Telling children as much of the truth as you can will help you build the communication blocks your family needs.

4. In situations when a child was sad because they missed their parent, I would say, "Oh, I'm sorry you're sad. I know what it's like to miss your mommy. When I was in school, I missed my mommy, too. Mommy's at work just like you're at school. When Mommy gets off work she will come to school and pick you up and take you home. Just like she does every day." Then I will say, "It's okay to miss Mommy. Just remember she is at work and will pick you up when she gets off!" Conversations like these, I have noticed, always soothe the child and seem to help them later when they miss their parents on another day.

You, too, can have these conversations with your child on days when you're at home with them or when you're driving in the car. I also find when you get to your destination you should (if your child is upset) remind them you have to go to work and will pick them up when you get off. Then leave. Under no circumstances should you stay, because your child will keep crying. Don't try to have these talks when you're almost at the place where you're dropping them off or right when you're leaving them if you haven't already had these conversations. Help them get ready by talking about these feelings when they feel safe with you at a time when you are not leaving.

Most of the time, though children's feelings are really fragile, they heal quickly with the right words and tone. I have also noticed that when I approached them in this way they appreciated that I took the time to address their feelings and that seemed to allow them to listen to my words.

# Typical Scenarios and Solutions at School

In this chapter, I want you to see how I interact with children at school in these stressful situations. You may find that many of the examples I give can help you and your child at home or in public situations, too. I want you to notice:

1. I don't lose my cool,

2. I have the confidence that my communication skills are healthy and work for the child, and

3. I am not focusing on me or my feelings—everything I do or say works toward correcting the problem in a teaching manner.

Doing 1, 2, and 3, I get the gift of sight, which means I see the outcome before it happens, as long as I understand how a child thinks. As the adults, you and I understand the bigger picture; if a child doesn't understand something we do, the way we handle them becomes our problem because it's our responsibility to help them along in this world. Their mistakes are necessary because they are the child's way into adulthood.

## Watch a Child Watch

Have you ever noticed how much children learn simply by observing? Here is a story of two-year-old Valerie. She was very interested in gymnastics, but she wasn't willing to do it because she didn't understand it and was very cautious. At two years old, this little girl could read at a first- or second-grade level, she was that smart. No matter what I said, no matter what I did, she was not going to try gymnastics until I explained why we did gymnastics. So I explained how gymnastics teaches us about our body and its limitations (what we can or can't do), and how to play safely. It could be that answering questions gives children the correct answer or resolves the importance of their "why" questions.

As I watched her watching other children, asking questions about what they were doing and why, I realized how important watching or observing is to a child *and* how important it is for adults to let children learn at their own pace. Another thing I find is that when you tell a child they can watch an event, rather than participate, it takes the pressure off them of having to do anything. If I had got upset at Valerie because she wouldn't participate, or handled her aggressively, she would have retreated from me and the class. See how important it is to handle children correctly and not be judgmental about their pace or effort? The lesson a parent might take from this is that sometimes when you offer your child an experience—like a dance class or series of art classes or even a playdate with a new person—they might need some time to watch before they can get involved. They might need to see it's okay for them to be there and you need to be ready to give them time. I find that with a little bit of patience and explanation, children will eventually become interested because they see other children having fun. I have never seen a situation in which a child forced to do something unwillingly has benefited from the activity.

Now some children cry when they enter my class because they don't know me or what's going on. They may have what I call transition or separation problems, meaning the child fears moving from one place or room to another. Parents, you may have a child who doesn't like to leave his room or his home, or his grandmother's home. They don't like change. Part of this reluctance may stem from the parent forgetting to build expectation in the child, or to communicate why the parent has to leave them at school or any other place. (See Part I) Sometimes it's because the child was having fun doing what they were doing and didn't want to be interrupted. In this situation, when a child is crying, I will pick the child up and hold them. Then I say, "Oh, you don't have to be sad. Everything is going to be okay." While I do this, I will pull out a chair, and tell the child they can watch. If after a few minutes the child still will not calm down, I don't have any other choice but to take the child back to his classroom and we will repeat the process the next week. You may not have that luxury in your situation, but it is definitely worthwhile to give the child a chance to become comfortable. that way the next time they will remember (or you can remind them) that you acknowledged their fear. Each time the child encounters the experience, the child feels more comfortable and is more likely to be willing to participate.

I have no problems with allowing the child to observe (as long as the child is not crying) because I know that when they are watching, they're learning, and they're learning to trust me. They are watching other children to see if anybody is getting hurt, to see my interactions with the children—for example, am I raising my voice unnecessarily?—and to see what the other children are doing.

So parents, even if you've paid for the art lesson and your child doesn't want to participate, don't get angry; she's probably still learning. When I'm teaching, my main objective is to get the child to do at least one thing: jump on the trampoline, go through the tunnel, go touch or sit on a mat—anything that gives me something to build on for the next time. With an unresponsive child, I'm waiting for them to take the lead and I am just following. I am always trying to get to a point to where the child will play with me. But I have to be very patient and open-minded to the fact that the child must have the will to want to try before I can get too involved. I find when I get involved too early, I get a bad result (like noncompliance and emotional response).

Children, from the very beginning, love their parents. To them, you are the greatest. So you can see how easy it is to disappoint them when they put you on such a pedestal. That's why I think it is vital that you let them know you make mistakes, too. I am the first to tell a child I made a mistake because I want them to know I am not perfect. I am not embarrassed about making a mistake. We all make mistakes but what you do after the mistake is where you build character. Yes, character. Letting your child see, hear, and know you made a mistake is okay as long as you let them know you should not have done that, or why you did it and apologize for your actions if need be.

Now, the following ways I try to get children involved might work for you as you play with your reluctant child, for example, on a playground or in a parent-and-child playgroup or at a school festivity. There are certain things that I do, like ask them questions about what the other children are doing. I ask them if they see children getting hurt. I ask them to look at the children's faces and to tell me if they have happy or sad faces. I ask them if they would like to participate. I tell them they do not have to do anything they do not want to do; they can just skip it and move to the next station or step. I also tell them that it is safe as long as I am helping, and if they need help, all they have to do is ask. I reassure them that their parent gave permission to play with me. A lot of the work with an unresponsive child is reassuring them, talking to them, and showing them that other children are playing and that they are having fun. The most important thing with an unresponsive child is to let them lead me. And when they're ready, I will be extremely cautious with them. I most definitely will not let myself get too far away from them because if they need me, I want to be right there. I don't want to be fifteen feet away so that I have to run over to the child. That may be too late. I follow them around my circuit until they feel comfortable enough that they can do it on their own. I will not help them unless they ask me to or unless I feel they could get hurt. I try to teach them to ask for my help instead of my just giving it. I find children learn faster if they are doing it on their own.

I never take their responses personally. I pay attention to their feelings, I listen to them, and I have patience when they are hesitant. This patience is especially necessary with children who are shy. In my classroom, this mainly happens with girls aged two to four years because the majority of their input has been from women (mom) and they can be intimidated by men. I understand this, so I play this little game of ignoring them. I let them see me, and I let them see that I see them. I leave it at that for the first few minutes because I realize if I make a lot of eye contact with them it scares them even more. At first, I will let the child watch and observe, and that careful dance can go on for up to two or three weeks. And that is absolutely okay. Until the child becomes comfortable with me, it doesn't matter what I say or do, the child will only become comfortable at their own pace and that pace is built on trust.

See how I chose to handle it. It is important to remember it is not about me. Letting a child be who they are and working around their discomfort is okay as long as you know what you are doing. Having a plan ahead about time of how to deal with your child is very important. Then when your child acts out, you don't have to get frustrated because you don't know what to do. You will already know. In almost all classroom scenarios, I need patience and must be ready to see the situation from a child's viewpoint. That is probably true for parents, too, when their child is disruptive or unresponsive. So you might need to be ready to pull out patience and a different viewpoint. I know with a little bit of my patience and understanding, a child who is scared or crying or disruptive can start to calm down and love me because they appreciate how I talk to and protect them.

When a child enters my class for the first time ready to have fun, I have a chance not only to change this child's life but also an opportunity to help them gain confidence and self-esteem through play and the words they will soon learn. Knowing the child is eager and ready to go and all I have to do is harness their energy makes my job much easier. Seeing the child excited about learning is magical. Not allowing them to get hurt in the process is priceless. Children love to get overexcited and it is my job to calm them back down so they can focus and listen. I do this by using my words, facial expressions, tones, kindness, and knowledge of the sport. I hope the following ideas will help you help your child as well.



In a new situation, a child may be hesitant but eager. As a child sees an adult take control, they begin to worry less and do more. When a child enters my class for the first time, I use the other children to demonstrate skills (or I will) as well as to show them how to repeat words I use to protect them and others from them. I find as the class goes on, the child starts to smile and engages because they feel safe; they can tell the other children are having fun and no one is getting hurt. Now, as this is going on, my main goal is to allow the child to experience a stress-free environment. I do this by saying, "If you do not want to do a skill, use your words and say, 'Coach, I don't want to do that!'" Give your child a chance to make his wishes known but still point out that other kids are having fun, not getting hurt or upset, and that the teacher is helping them.

Keeping things simple and at a pace the children are comfortable with is what works best for them. I continuously engage with them by cheering them on and praising them a lot when they accomplish skills. I also say, "Trust Coach Bruce; he won't let me fall" while the children are taking turns. I constantly remind them, "If there is something you don't know how to do and want to try, tell me and I will help you!" Encourage your child in the same way by saying, "I could help you or maybe the teacher would help you." Praise the effort they are making in the art class or dance class.

To sum up: see how adults just looking at things a little differently can make a world of difference for children. See how my influence and understanding of situations determined the outcome to be positive for the child. See how if I had handled it incorrectly and taken it personally, these children most likely would never have wanted anything to do with the experience or me.

By allowing children to make decisions based on what they see and hear, I give them control, the chance to make choices, and a voice so they can tell me. One of the reasons this works so well is because I do not allow a child to fear me or the physical activity. It is through these simple, respectful, patient actions that the children learn to respect me and others. They love me and thrive in my class. They remember those classes, and, in later years, will stop me on the street to thank me for allowing them to be in my class. This way of thinking and speaking works, and works well, so just keep trying. It will come.

*I am growing up quickly. It must be very difficult for you to keep pace with me, but please try.*

Children keep you on your toes. They make you do things you don't want to do. They can upset you because you are trying so hard to raise a good, healthy child. But please keep trying and just know your child will appreciate it one day. I hope this insight will help you calm down and realize you can be a great parent. You now have insight you didn't have before and you are making a big effort by reading this book. So keep learning and get a plan so you can be available for your child in a way that is healthy for you and for  them.

# A Coach's Attitude

As I've said throughout this book, children think differently than adults. Although you may think your child understands your words and your feelings, they don't. And if you think they do, they're just mimicking your words. So most of the time, they're reacting to your tone, facial expressions, even body postures in a completely different way than you mean them. In the following short scenarios, I want you to immerse yourself in the child's point of view—as if they could tell you what they really think or feel. And then read my response to that viewpoint—what I have learned in my years of watching children, talking to children, teaching children, and disciplining children.

## A Child's Point of View on Life and Discipline

**I know quite well I should not get all I ask for. I'm only testing.**

Spoiling a child disrupts their sense of boundaries, making them selfish and teaching them how to test you. They lose the value of what it is to earn something. And, unfortunately, you are creating a monster for the rest of us to deal with. Children should have limitations and should be taught not to ask for everything. Let the child know when a gift or treat is possible and when something must be earned. For example, before you leave for the grocery store, explain to your child where you are going and why: you are going for food and supplies and this is not a time for gifts, toys, or candy. When you spoil or bribe a child you are teaching them how to test you. When it is time for them to get a treat, I suggest you tell them beforehand. I always try to let children know as soon as I know so it can help them prepare as well.

**Be firm with me. I prefer it. It makes me feel more secure and it will help me to stop testing so much.**

If you are wishy-washy, your children will pick up on it and start to become very emotional (whiny). They will test you because they don't know where their, and your, boundaries are. Children rely on you for consistency in your behavior so they can learn from you. When you are firm with your children, they know their boundaries and feel reassured. They know that you are serious.

**Keep me from forming bad habits (flinching, mimicking, odd physical movements, lying, etc.). I have to rely on you to detect them in my early stages.**

If you let children form bad habits, it's harder for you to break these habits later on. Children don't understand what "bad habits" are. When they see someone else do it, they don't know they're not supposed to do it until they've tried it. Sometimes a child may experiment with a behavior to see what kind of response he'll get from you. Don't jump to conclusions, but if it becomes a habit, immediately speak to your child about why some behaviors are not socially acceptable. Remember, children are visual learners.

**Please don't make me feel smaller than I am. It only makes me behave "stupidly big."**

Children already have a hard enough time dealing with being young. They are always trying to act older or be bigger. That's why children always talk about their age. For example, "I am almost five, when I turn five I will be bigger," or "I am growing and soon I'll be bigger." So when you talk to them like you did when they were babies, your child will try to behave like they are bigger or older, usually to bad endings.

**When you have to correct me, I will listen better if you talk quietly to me in private.**

The more respect I give children the more respect they give me. Also, if I embarrass a child in front of others I do not have 100% of the child's attention and the child gets upset, angry, and hurt; then I have to deal with their pain. I get a better result when I speak to a child in private and it seems that the child does appreciate me for this. Plus it will help children be more mindful of the people around them.

**It upsets my sense of values when you make me feel that my mistakes are a big deal. Then I feel sorry for myself.**

A mistake is just a mistake, nothing more. Do not place too high a value on mistakes. Mistakes are how we all learn and are a part of life. When a child makes a mistake, don't treat it too harshly. I look at it as an opportunity to help and teach, to show your child how patient and willing to help you are. This is a great time to show your child you can be calm, but you don't have to be soft. Use child's currency. Just remember, when your child makes a mistake, this is a great time for you to correct the problem and bond with your child.

**Please don't protect me from all consequences. Sometimes I need to learn the hard (painful) way.**

Being overprotective can actually hurt your child because they learn to count on you more than they should. Children need to learn about life through their own mistakes and experiences, and learn the consequences for those choices. It's *your* choice when you are overprotective.

**Sometimes I'll act out or become silly just for attention.**

I find children like to see if I am paying attention and so they act out or become silly (acting silly is just being a child). They test by making little mistakes to see if I will catch it. Children like knowing you are paying attention and it is okay when they do this because this is your time to let them know you are paying attention. You do this is by correcting them when they do test you for attention. (This is not experimenting.)

**If you nag me, I will have to protect myself by appearing deaf, especially if I am playing a sport or having fun.**

Children do this when you step across their boundaries. They signal that they want to be left alone. Sometimes children pretend deafness because you do it to them. If children continuously feel they are not being heard, this is a way for them to get even. Lastly, I find some children do this because they are not paying attention to their surroundings and are living in their own world. This just means they are young.

**I feel badly let down when promises are broken.**

I find the worst thing I can do is tell a child I am going to do something and not follow through with it. I have noticed that when this happens, children get their feelings hurt, and most of the time, they think they did something wrong. That is why I never make rash promises. I also get the feeling when I let a child down they get disappointed and slowly stop trusting me. Or worse, when I do make a promise they are less likely to believe or trust me.

**I cannot explain myself as well as I would like, especially when I am scared and so I am not always very accurate.**

Please, parents, remember that when a child is scared and you are aggressive—you scream, threaten, or spank your child—he or she is not capable of answering questions under those circumstances. Also, children are trying to learn what your words really mean. Even if a child is familiar with a word, they still are not capable of understanding the full meaning of the word. They only understand the parts that pertain to them in their world. So if you want your child to answer you, he cannot be scared and if he answers, you should understand that he is mimicking words he thinks you want to hear.

**I am easily frightened into telling lies.**

When you confront your child about a possible lie, you have to do it carefully. Children are still learning and it will help them so much if you don't press them too hard or be over aggressive about their honesty because they are still figuring out how to put the action to words and put the words together. Can't cope? What you should do is let them know that because you are the parent it is important for you to know so you can show, tell, and teach them why we don't lie.

**When you are inconsistent, I get confused and I lose faith in you.**

Consistency is what makes a parent trustworthy. Showing a child that your words, behavior, and attitude are consistent will help them in every part of their lives, but when you are inconsistent, your child has no other choice but to test. They test boundaries, punishment, or fairness looking for and hoping for consistency. Given the choice, most children would choose consistency so they can learn how to predict what you might do or say.

**If you put me off when I ask questions I may stop asking and start seeking my information elsewhere.**

Children are constantly looking for attention and they get this through asking questions. Questions are how humans learn and build our brains, but more important, children find out how interested you are in them by the way you answer their questions. When I get involved in a child's question it creates something I call "love." Because I love each and every child their questions are important to me. I want each child to know that by always answering their questions and by continually asking them questions. I do this because I want to teach each child how to learn how to ask questions and to let them know questions are how we find out the right and wrong answer. Children get disappointed easily. And if you leave it up to someone else to answer your child's questions, he or she may not get the answers you would give. So please take the time to answer your child's questions.

**My fears are terribly real to me and you can help me much more if you try to understand rather than tell me they are silly.**

Once I learned to stop making children do things they were afraid to do, I was amazed at how fast a child was able to overcome his or her fear. This happened because I not only acknowledged the child's feeling, but I was also able to explain how I would help and protect them. I also let the child take her time to become comfortable. Once the child saw I wasn't going to force them, it helped them hear me and trust me.

**Please don't ever suggest that you are infallible. It gives me too great a shock when I discover that you are not.**

Children from the very beginning love their parents. To them, you are the greatest. So you can see how easy it is to disappoint them when they put you on such a pedestal. That's why I think it is vital that you let them know you make mistakes, too. I am the first to tell a child I made a mistake because I want them to know I am not perfect. I am not embarrassed about making a mistake. We all make mistakes but what you do after the mistake is where you build character. Yes, character. Letting your child see, hear, and know you made a mistake is okay as long as you let them know you should not have done that, or why you did it and to apologize for your actions if need be.

**Listen to me. I have a lot to say. I need you to be patient with me because I am still learning.**

Children really like it when you listen to them because it makes them feel important or that what they have to say is interesting to you. Children are always looking for attention and this is a safe way to show it to them and learn about them. Learning how to listen to a child is how I learned so much about them.

**I do not understand the concept of "time" and other adult concepts. If I give the impression I do then just know I am mimicking behavior or words.**

I find the more I understand what children do and don't understand, the more likely I am to get my point across. In today's world adults need an instant pay-off and we call it "Time Out!" Try to keep the "time-outs" to a small amount of time: the more I try to explain the reason for my actions, the fewer "time-outs" I need. Being consistent in your discipline will stop your child from testing so much. In addition, children can't see the big picture of why you are doing what you are doing so other adult concepts are not on their radar. Now what I mean by that is if your child doesn't understand this concept there is a great chance they don't understand (as an example) reasoning, being responsible, or what having to work for a living mean.

**When it comes to discipline, keep repeating yourself; it reassures me.**

Repeating behavior allows the child to start to predict my actions and helps them start the thinking process. When I repeat certain behavior, it not only reassures the child, but it also lets them know what I will accept and what I will not. Having them repeat your words when explaining things to them is the key to the beginning of this process. Everything starts with having each child learn how to repeat words. Then when I repeat discipline, it ties everything together.

**If you talk to me as you would to any other child, you will always get a better result.**

Sometimes I wish I could tell parents this in hopes that it will ease the pressure of being a parent. Just because your child is stressing you doesn't give you the right to act aggressively. Children are still learning and I find it helps them to learn faster when I am patient, loving, and respectful. I find the more respect I give to a younger child the more respectful they are to me. It's because of the way I talk to them.

**When you yell, threaten, or spank (hit) me I get scared, then mad. I stop thinking about what I did and start thinking about what you just did.**

This is the reason children get mad at you for punishing them. If they can't understand the reason you are punishing them, then how you are choosing to do it isn't working at all. Children need to understand that when they make a mistake or break a rule *that* is the reason you are getting involved. If you continually think your child understands the way you are treating them then just know you are raising a scared child. I think it is important for you to know this because this is how I will get you to change the way you look at disciplining your children. If you look through my eyes you can see that handling your child's feelings about scaring them must be addressed first. Then you can explain why you got involved. If this process doesn't take place as part of discipline, I believe your child does not understand you and will become afraid of you.

**When you scare me, I will say things like "I don't know," "He (or she) did it." I'll shrug my shoulders, or I will give you a blank stare.**

When children say or do these things it tells me I need to apologize for scaring them so they don't think I am being mean or attacking them. Then I tell them why I got involved and why I need them to stop by using child's currency and explaining to them again why I got involved. Remember, consistency will help with this a lot as well as not having your child fear you.

**Talking down to me makes me very emotional but most of all it makes me not like you.**

When you talk down to your child you are really hurting your child's feelings and making them feel like their efforts aren't good enough. That will lower their confidence or self-esteem. It also causes them to feel sorry for themselves and they become less likely to want your help or input. I can say from experience, nothing good ever comes of speaking down to a child. When this happens everything you do with this child becomes very emotional. Everything that happens now is done through fear and guessing.

**I couldn't get on without experimenting, so please put up with it.**

There is a difference between a child experimenting and a child misbehaving. The difference is the child is interested in what they are doing and *interested in my reaction (experimenting) rather than being scared of getting into trouble (misbehaving)*. When a child experiments I can usually tell by the expression they have on their face as well as by the way they react to you when you question what they are doing. I find experimenting is testing to see if I'm paying attention, or trying to see if they like something, or following what someone else did. Experimenting is not misbehaving and, in my opinion, should not be punished. This is how all children learn. You should talk about the experience with your child.

**I thrive with lots of understanding and love, but then I don't need to tell you that, do I?!**

Because I praise children a lot, they gain confidence and self-esteem. The more praise I give to a child, the more respect or better attention I get back. The more understanding I am of children's experiments and tests and the less time spent punishing, the faster the children rebound. I find parents are so overwhelmed that sometimes they can be overbearing. My attitude is to teach rather than scold. Telling children "I love you" is not enough; you have to show them by being involved in their lives through love and understanding of their needs.

**Your support lets me know you are interested in what I am doing.**

Support to a child is like money to you. This is what every child wants from you. Support is how you show your child you approve of what they are doing and agree with the choices they are making. It tells your child you are interested in what's going on in their life. Through questions you can show your child support even if you can't be there. If you support your child in what they are doing, it is a confidence and self-esteem builder for every child. Children need support and you are the best one to give it to them.

**Please keep asking me questions about my daily life, lots of questions. It is how you teach me about engaging.**

One way to engage in your child's life is simply by asking questions. Children find a lot of comfort in this engagement because it allows them to tell you what's going on with their own words and lets the child dictate how much they want to let me know. You get the opportunity to show you care, you are interested, and you are proud of them.

**I am growing up quickly. It must be very difficult for you to keep pace with me, but please try.**

Children keep you on your toes. They make you do things you don't want to do. They can upset you because you are trying so hard to raise a good, healthy child. But please keep trying and just know your child will appreciate it one day. I hope this insight will help you calm down and realize you can be a great parent. You now have insight you didn't have before and you are making a big effort by reading this book. So keep learning and get a plan so you can be available for your child in a way that is healthy for you and for them.

---

I would like to get your feedback on *The Gymnastics of Love & Discipline*. I plan to revise this book as often as necessary to keep my readers as current as possible.

I will be traveling the country giving seminars and lectures to present first-hand how I interact with children. The intent is to create debate in this country about how we parent our children to help parents choose a  more positive approach.

When giving me feedback I hope you'll consider questions like these:

- Did I help you to understand your child better?
- Does this knowledge make you think differently than you did before? How so?
- What piece of information helped you the most?
- What discipline techniques did you stop using after you read this book?
- Did you find any of the information confusing or unworkable?
- Please share any word patterns you found to be useful.
- Please share any tests you did that proved to you that your child didn't understand you or your actions when you thought they did.

I will post your thoughts and feedback on my website along with my responses so I can continue to provide workable methods.

Here are ways you can contact me:

**www.CoachBruceBenko.com, or**
**www.TheGymnasticsofLoveAndDiscipline.com**

# PART III

## Resources & References

## Teachers' Wish List

I mentioned earlier that I spoke with certified, veteran teachers at HeartsHome who worked directly under Dr. Kay Albrecht and Carla Gwinn, asking them a lot of questions and gaining their input for this book. What follows is a letter I sent to them asking these two questions: If there was one thing you could change about the parent-child-teacher relationship, what would it be? And if you could change something in the way a parent deals with their child, what would it be?

A summary of their responses follows, as well as a thoughtful wish list—things they wish they could say to parents that would make the children's lives better as well as help the teachers perform better.

> *Dear Teachers & Educators,*
>
> *This book is about giving back to the children by teaching parents how to give their children a voice as well as letting parents know that raising a child should focus on consistency, accountability, and patience, not the parents' feelings.*
>
> *Every single one of you has inspired me by your dedication to education and children, and I would like your input in this area. This is a chance for you to give back—and I hope get back—as well. Feel free to take your time and please try to keep your answer under 150 words. If I have your permission and I believe in your words, I will add your contribution to this book.*
>
> *Thank you. Coach*

After reading their responses, I was amazed that they all said basically the same thing. They wanted the parent to be more involved in the child's school and schoolwork, and wanted the parent to be on the same page as the teacher, meaning they should follow the teacher's lead and schedule so the child didn't get confused.

The troubling part for me was that the teachers said they would do the work with the child mentally and emotionally, but when the child went home, the parents wouldn't stay consistent. The teachers also felt it was mainly because the parents weren't engaging with them.

For example, the teachers wanted parents to ask more questions about what their children were learning. Parents could show more interest in what their child is doing at school by getting involved in the P.T.A., meeting the directors or principals, asking questions, and showing the people who are teaching your child that you care.

Just remember when you neglect these things, your child suffers the consequences by possibly slipping through the cracks.

After hearing their responses, I thought it would be a good idea to have an assortment of teachers help me compile a list of activities, ideas, and attitudes that would help parents understand better how they could make teachers' jobs easier. This list was compiled and discussed with numerous educators throughout my career.

## Teachers' Wish List

**I wish parents** would understand how important it is for your child to see you involved in their school and schoolwork.

**I wish parents** could see from our point of view how positively their child reacts when their parents do get involved with school stuff.

**I wish parents** could understand that if they knew what their child was learning or doing at school, it would give their child a better opportunity for success, especially the child who is having a hard time with a certain subject. (See what you're missing!)

**I wish parents** could understand how important school is to a child's life. For parents not to be involved should scare them to death.

**I wish parents** would volunteer at least once or twice a year for something at their child's school. (For example, P.T.A., be a teacher's helper for a day, ask to chaperone a field trip.)

**I wish parents** would offer to help their child's teacher once in a while. Does the teacher need supplies, or how can I help my child in your class?

**I wish parents** would bring their child to school on time so as not to disrupt our day.

**I wish parents** would talk to their children more about leaving them at school instead of just dropping them off. Children need to understand why their parents are leaving, when they'll return, and to be assured that they'll return on time.

**I wish parents** would talk to each other: find out who their child's friends' are, meet the friends' parents, basically be more sociable.

**I wish parents** would understand school is a lot more than just academic education. It's socializing, it's creating friendships, it's learning how to follow rules, it's so many things. So for you not to be a big part of that causes us concern.

**I wish parents** would stop expecting us to teach their children how to behave or show respect. Our jobs are to inspire and teach.

**I wish parents** would get involved in their child's schooling because it would make our already incredibly hard jobs a lot easier.

**I wish parents** would help their child with homework so the child's work is always finished even if it isn't always correct. If the child has an interaction with the parent as he works on the assignment, he's better prepared when the teacher goes over it in class.

**I wish parents** would understand we as teachers love our job and for you to think anything less . . . well, that's just unacceptable.

**I wish you** knew how hard school is nowadays and how much is required of your child. To have little or no help from mom and dad makes it almost impossible for them to succeed. If I didn't have twenty-plus other students, I would be happy to help your child more.

**I wish you** could see the look on children's faces when they see another parent show up to help their child. We find children are very polite when someone's parent shows up to help.

**I wish you** would be more patient with me as well, and don't forget
your child is not the only one in my class. Sometimes you
make us feel like your child is more important than another.
Just remember: help us help you.

**I wish parents** would be consistent with the discipline they give their
children. Both parents should be on the same page.

**I wish parents** wouldn't make excuses as to why children are
perpetually late or haven't finished their homework.

**I wish parents** gave their children a strict bedtime. It's important for
them to be well rested.

**I wish parents** would ask about my teaching and discipline
techniques and use those with their children at home.

**I wish parents** wouldn't resort to always using corporal punishment on
their children as a discipline technique. It shows children that it
is always okay to hit someone when they do something wrong.

**I wish parents** of divorced children wouldn't bad-mouth each other in
front of their children. Please take the time to explain what's
going on and that the children are still loved.

**I wish parents** would let the teachers know if there is anything
unusual going on at home so the teachers can be prepared for
any different behavior from the children.

**I wish parents** would take criticism of their children well and
understand that the teachers are only trying to make better
humans of their children.

**I wish parents** wouldn't use phrases like "boys will be boys" because
this gives boys the excuse they need to act up.

**I wish parents** wouldn't nitpick about every scrape or bruise their child gets because most of the time even the children don't know how they got them.

**I wish parents** would teach their children proper table manners at home so they can assimilate at school better. It is not the teacher's job to feed children ages three and up.

**I wish parents** wouldn't hold teachers responsible for toys their children bring to school and get lost or stolen. Do not send toys to school with your children unless you are prepared for this.

**I wish parents** would push their children to do better.

**I wish parents** would understand that having a well-disciplined child is just as important as, or more important than, having a smart child.

**I wish parents** would help their children be more independent. For example, they should begin to dress themselves and clean up after themselves no later than three years of age.

Parents, you can see that these teachers, and, I believe, most teachers, want to give each child as much attention and even love as they can. They need all the help you can give them and that help comes from your consistent, patient, encouraging parenting. Let's work together to help our children do better in school. This insight can help you help us help them. Now that you have these wishes don't be afraid to ask questions. Remember to use The Power.

# The Importance of Developing
# Motor Skills Early in Life

I believe that if gross motor skills are not acquired and developed at an early age, children will have a hard time with rhythm, timing, tempo, coordination and balance later in life. Also, I find as children get older they lose confidence and self-esteem to do things that require them to have skill through movement, especially sports like gymnastics.

I have also noticed as children get older they lose the ability to put together more than three skills in a row like hop step, skip step, jump step or run, jump and roll. They can do one or two but the third, fourth and fifth cause confusion, whereas a child who has a physical background that emphasized gross motor skills can do five or sometimes more actions in a row.

I believe this deterioration occurs because the brain is not developing the ability to teach itself early enough, and when the body is required to perform such tasks later, when children become nine or ten years old, the brain sends a series of signals out and the body receives confusing directions. The brain's neurons are no longer connected because of the lack of stimulation. Then children feel afraid and the child becomes less inclined to continue to try (so again, he loses confidence, then self-esteem). We are now learning that when the mind doesn't get the correct stimulation through programs that enhance gross motor development, neurons that aren't being stimulated eventually die off and can cause problems for your child mentally and physically later in life.

One of the studies that helped prove this for me refers to the brain as making a phone call, meaning wanting a body part to move. To get the correct response you want that signal to ring only at the designated place. In other words, you don't want many phones to start ringing in every house between here and there. You want the one phone only to ring so you can reach the person you wanted to talk to, i.e., get the correct movement. Our brains work the same way, and in order for this process to work your brain has to start killing off the neurons that aren't giving you the correct response so the right response can be connected.

Recent studies have discovered the brain works and learns through the dying off and growing of neurons. Our brains keep growing until we reach the age of thirty, but that doesn't mean we can relearn things once our brains are set.

## Setting the Mind, Making a Picture

I have always believed we have only a limited time to set our minds. Once that time has passed, our brains are set and are not capable of learning some things like rhythm, timing, tempo, coordination, and balance later in life. (I believe this affects our equilibrium.)

I have watched thousands of children who had a gross motor background perform from the ages of two to thirteen years of age (some children to the age of eighteen) perform. They were more active and showed considerable difference from children who were not exposed to this type of program until later in life. Children with balance and coordination not only had greater confidence and higher self-esteem but it seemed that because they could do these things with their bodies, *they could do most anything else.*

I could never figure out why children who were eight and up couldn't pick up simple skills that other children were doing at age four or five. (And it was not because they got physically bigger. That had only a small effect.) I would put considerable time and effort into helping those older children grow on a gross motor scale—which included gymnastics—and I found they could only achieve to a certain level of development.

Three recent studies might suggest an answer. One of these studies was done on mice by Dr. Jeffrey Lichtman, who showed how a part of the brain learns and works. A second study and a documentary called the "Science of Babies" done by National Geographic show how children grow and what part the environment plays. A third study was done on a girl found fastened from birth to the age of thirteen to a toilet in a small room by her handicapped and mentally ill parents. She got little to no stimulation or engagement. (All studies were published in 2007/8. See reference page for website information on each study.)

## Lichtman Study

The study of mice showed actual computer images of the brain and how neurons die and grow. During this process, neurons that were not being stimulated through the learning process eventually died and the neurons that were being used properly grew: they sent the signal and got the correct response. The study claims that the brain sets itself and once it does, it is set for life, even in injury. But if injury occurs before the brain sets, many problems will occur, which if not corrected, will affect an individual later in life. Please take time to watch a video of this study on the website. It will give you a lot of insight.

## National Geographic Study

I believe we human beings become different mentally and socially within our environments. No environment is the same, and our individual experiences in those individual environments are what tie together the ability to become an individual. I urge you to watch a television program called "Science of Babies" produced by the National

Geographic Channel. This program is a study done on children from infancy through two years and is one of the latest on the effects the environment plays in children's development as well as how we learn from what is in our environment.

As we begin to grow, our environment—and what we can do in it—constantly changes. In this study, you will learn there are three different stages of learning our minds and bodies have to go through before the body and mind can set themselves. Keep in mind as you read through the stages that at each stage, the baby has to learn everything all over again. Stage 1 is infancy to six months. At this stage of development, the mind and body are trying to learn how to work together by killing off certain neurons in the brain so the correct body part will work according to the thought. (This is why babies involuntarily shake when they are infants.) Now as the child goes through this stage, the people around them control nearly everything in the infant's environment until the child can take some control, which is when the child starts to crawl.

Stage 2 is six months to one year old. At this stage, the child becomes mobile and starts to learn through pain and experience as he explores a larger environment (under normal circumstances). They learn from everything in their environment. As they grow, the mind takes in more of the environment, but because the baby hasn't reached its full potential of growth (being able to walk or run), it has to learn its boundaries and capabilities all over again through trial and error.

Stage 3, where the child learns how to walk, then run, is the stage at which the mind starts to remember by setting itself after Stage 3 because the body is receiving the correct signals and getting the correct body part to move. Since this is where we reach our full potential (mobility) the mind will now set itself.

Since our environment dictates what we can learn, and because I was able to control a small piece of my students' classroom environment, I was able to see how a child learned. I watched children gain confidence and self-esteem as well as discovered when or if a child became fearful and withdrawn strictly based on this environment. Because I see so many things a child gains in my controlled environment, I believe that the child can also lose so many things in a bad or unsafe environment. Just because you are at home with your child doesn't mean your environment is completely safe. The people you know and the energy they bring into your child's environment affects your child. Pay close attention to your child's environment and who you let in it. Your child learns everything from his environment. Remember, one of the biggest reasons children can become angry, frustrated, happy, or sad is directly associated with their environment.

When I saw this firsthand, it made me think a lot more carefully before I lightly introduced something or someone into a child's environment, which in turn made me think more about each child.

## Susan "Genie" Wiley

Several years ago, a study was done on a thirteen-year-old girl who had been deprived of virtually everything a child needs to survive outside of food. She was locked in a room where she was attached to a toilet by a belt for most of her life, with very little engagement from her mentally ill parents. Once this girl was discovered, doctors, psychiatrists and physical therapists did studies of her development. Even after many years of therapy, she was never able to make complete sentences. She would point and say, "Want," or point at something and say, "Mine" and protect that object. Once her mind was set, the doctors concluded that, because of the lack of stimulation and environmental growth when she was young, she would never acquire the ability to speak complete sentences or advance any further developmentally. (Watch this program. It will blow you away!)

Also look for a study called "The Girl in the Window." This girl was found at age six in similar circumstances to the Wiley child. You might think that because she was only six, she would be able to learn more than the older child, but the lack of engagement and stimulation from parents kept her from learning just as it had "Genie."

I believe people should know it is important for all children to be exposed to some kind of physical developmental program such as gymnastics, dance, or karate, because not only will it help them physically and mentally grow but this exposure will aoso stimulate their ability to gain confidence, which stimulates self-esteem. I can't stress enough how important gross motor development is to a child, but I can show you a child who doesn't have it. There are studies that prove on a learning scale if you don't use it, you lose it, and lose it forever.

## Results

As the years have passed, I believe our society has allowed most kids to do just enough to get by developmentally, meaning they can execute the basic skills: run, jump, climb, hop, etc. But when you ask them to put skills together with rhythm, timing, or tempo, that's where you lose most children. Since most kids are not in athletic programs at school or after-school physical programs like skating, swimming, gymnastics, biking, karate, or dancing, they just don't get the stimulation they need. I evaluate my students by asking them to complete more than three skills in a row. When I test a child who has not been exposed to a gross motor development program, the difference is like night and day. But what can I say to those parents? They have jobs to go to and house payments and carpools. They think they're doing right by their children. So many children go home to sit on their behinds in front of a computer or a television and by the time they're thirteen, they're almost as badly harmed as the thirteen-year old tied to a toilet all her life. Their brains are set and they may struggle the rest of their lives to have the confidence and self-esteem that physical coordination can give them. I believe our brains build a picture or set the mind at an early age. Gross motor development is as essential as any other part of a child's early childhood development. Remember the expression "set in your ways"? Well, I believe this rings true when it comes to gross motor development. The majority of our children never receive the proper gross motor development training early enough and once the mind sets, it's over.

The last point about gross motor development is this: during the early years, a child is looking for confidence and self-esteem. Through gross motor development, a child gets an abundance of both and it will completely change a child's life just by having the attitude "I did it!"

# Resources, References, and
# Website Addresses

1. Baumrind, Diana (1996) "A blanket injunction against disciplining, Use of spanking is not warranted by the data." *Pediatrics*, October, 828-832. Regents of University of California, 1111 Franklin St., Oakland, CA 94607
   www.universityofcalifornia.edu/news/article/3518

   This article states that there is no lasting harm among adolescents from "moderate" spanking in childhood. Its main point is that it is the intensity of the discipline, rather than to hit or not to hit that affects the child. The article also found that intense verbal discipline is just as harmful as intense spanking. It is the overall style of discipline that is most important. The article supports the author's statements that discipline should involve teaching in a loving way. It supports the author's statements about an adult's tone of voice being as importantas, or more important than, the words spoken.

2. Delaney, Kathleen (1999) "Time Out: An overused and misused milieu intervention." *Journal of Child and Adolescent Psychiatric Nursing.* April-June: 53
   www3.interscience.wiley.com/journal/119938862/abstract

   This study states that "time outs" can become ineffective when used so often that they become automatic. The use of "time out" can also be misused when the amount of time is too long. This study supports what the author believes about this style of discipline. Its findings state that "time out" is only useful when the amount of time is short and when the technique is not used very often.

3. Graziano, Anthony, M. et al (1996). "Subabusive violence in child rearing in middle-class American families." *Pediatrics*, October: 845-849
www.pediatrics.aappublications.org/cgi/content/abstract/98/4/845
The abstract of this article may be viewed free of charge, but reader must pay a small fee to read entire article.

It reports the effect of a long-term study of spanking in middle-class American families in order to determine whether the use of spanking should be reduced or eliminated. The term "subabusive" means the use of hitting or spanking that does not leave a mark on the child, or that is less than the standard meaning of "abuse." The study involved 320 families. The parents studied grew up mainly in the 1960s and 1970s and their children were born in the 1980s. The study supports statements and opinions of the author on styles of discipline and how effective—or ineffective—they are. It supports the author's view that discipline should be through teaching.

4. Hyman, Irwin A. (1997). *The Case Against Spanking*. San Fransisco. Jossy-Bass, Inc.
www.eric.ed.gov/ERICWebPortal/recordDetail?accno=ED423500

This study supports the argument against the use of spanking and supports the opinions of the author. It supports the use of other forms of discipline and distinguishes between assertiveness and aggression. Ordering information can be found on the site for those who wish to purchase the entire work.

5. Reibstein, Larry, and Susan Miller. "The debate over discipline." *Newsweek*. Spring/Summer 1997: 64-66.
www.newsweek.com/id/95379

This article is supportive of the author's view of spanking as ineffective in the long term. The article relates several practical situations with young children.

6. Windell, James (1991). Discipline: A Sourcebook of 50 Failsafe Techniques For Parents. New York: Collier.
A related website: www.irvingisd.net/townley/Newsletters/November%202002%20English.pdf

Has a very useful newsletter for those interested.

7. Highly useful and informative websites and links:
www.childhelp.org

This site has so many subpages and helpful links that a reader could easily become lost in it for many days, finding multiple sources, lists, and links

with help for parents, teachers, and others. Once on the homepage, a reader should find the tab marked "About Abuse" and then click on the menu item "Helpful Links."
Some of these links are summarized below:
Center for Effective Parenting: www.parenting-ed.org

Information on this site supports the author's arguments for establishing proper communication with children, mind set and influence of early experiences, the parent as a role model, use of praise, respect, consistency, listening to children and using/misusing promises. A reader may download many free worksheets and tip sheets on a variety of topics in PDF format. All topics are highly practical, useful, and supportive of the philosophy related in this book.

Child Care Aware: www.childcareaware.org

This site has many resources for parents to locate good childcare centers and programs.

Child Trends Data Bank: www.childtrendsdatabank.org

This site lists many studies and reports which support the philosophy stated in this book. It is especially helpful in searching for study results of groups of children in pre-K through grade three.

Circle of Parents: www.circleofparents.org

This site tells parents how to locate a support group in their area. One article, "To Discipline Means to Teach," supports the techniques stated in this book. Readers may download and print any of a large collection of tip sheets and helpful hints on a variety of topics of discipline: choice, handling tantrums, swearing, teen issues, and many more.

New Parents Network: www.newparentsnetwork.org

This site is an umbrella for resources for parents, especially parents of infants. Many good parenting tips and resources are listed, as well as links to other sources and organizations.

Stand For Children: www.stand.org

Zero to Three: www.zerotothree.org

The stated mission of this site is to inform and educate people about children from birth to three years. It promotes good health and development (physical, social and emotional) for children in these crucial early years. There are sections on brain research during this age as well as free down-loadable hand-outs in PDF format in English and Spanish. One especially useful article (on the home page, click on "Key Topics" and locate "Brain Development" on the left side of the page in a menu bar), "Starting Smart," relates research information related to neglect and abuse. The studies relate that children who are abused and neglected in the early years may suffer serious difficulties in school and may not be as intelligent as they might have been if not abused or neglected. The results indicate that a child's brain loses some of its "plasticity" after age ten. This may indicate that while children may grow, learn, and change after that time, some areas of learning will be much more difficult. The study also describes the effects of trauma and stress on the young child.

This site is a "must see" resource for parents and caretakers of very young children.

8. The Learning Channel: www.tlc.com

A search of "Wild Child" will lead the reader to various studies on severely abused and neglected children, the fragility of a child's brain, and related information.

9. The study of Susan "Genie" Wiley, a thirteen-year-old girl discovered in 1970 who was mentally and physically abused by her mentally ill parents. Her developmental delay is mentioned in this book. www.countryhistorian.com/cecilweb/index.php/Genie-Wiley

This site gives the basic outline of this child's tragic life. While most of the actual details of the studies of her are not available to the public through the internet, a determined individual may travel to the UCLA Library, where the documents are housed under restricted access. One apparent reason for discontinuing the research is that the researchers involved became the child's foster parents. This apparently breached scientific protocols for objective study. The site does state that the child, now an adult, lives in a home for the mentally retarded.

10. Another case came to light recently about a child named "Dani" who faced the kind of deprivation that the Wiley girl did. For information see the following link: www.tampabay.com/features/humaninterest/article750838.ece

11. Jean Blades Madigan, author, workshop presenter, and educator, website: www.actionbasedlearning.com Information on the site, books, and products available uphold the author's statements that balance, coordination, and cognitive learning are enhanced by physical movement. Teachers who have attended the workshops report

that they were given many practical activities that enhance academic achievement through physical activity.

**Other related websites with good information for early childhood education and related themes:**

12. National Association for the Education of Young Children: www.naeyc.org

   This national organization promotes developmentally appropriate practices for educating young children. Many day care centers are members—an indication of a good day care provider. The organization has lots of information to offer, holds conferences, and offers books on many subjects related to its mission.

13. Houston Area Association for the Education of Young Children: www.haaeyc.org

   Houston, Texas, chapter of the national organization with similar goals and mission for the greater Houston area. Many other major cities and states serve as local branches of NAEYC.

14. Innovations in Early Childhood Education, Dr. Kay Albrecht: www.innovationsinece.com

   This site has excellent information that supports the author's philosophy. The organization was founded by one of the author's mentors.

15. Randy Pausch's Last Lecture: www.randypausch.com

   Scroll down to the seventy-six-minute lecture (you will be directed to youtube.com) and hear this very upbeat man discuss living with cancer. It will be an inspiration. After all, it is addressed to his children right before he dies.

16. Discovery Channel: www.discoverychannel.com

   Wealth of information on many more topics than children and discipline.

17. National Geographic Channel: www.natgeotv.com

   Search for "Science of Babies" and "Science of the Brain" for interesting research studies and information.

---

# Bibliography of Related Books

17. Lawlis, Frank, Ph.D., *Mending the Broken Bond: The 90-Day Answer to Repairing Your Relationship with Your Child.* New York: Plume, 2008.

18. Lawlis, Frank, Ph.D. *The Stress Answer: Train Your Brain to Conquer Depression and Anxiety in 45 Days.* New York: Viking Press, 2008.

19. Madigan, Jean Blaydes, *Thinking on Your Feet.* Book is available only through the website:
www.actionbasedlearning.com